Macaulay

Owen Dudley Edwards

Macaulay

St. Martin's Press
New York

All rights reserved. For information, write:
Scholarly and Reference Division,
St. Martin's Press, Inc., 175 Fifth Avenue, New York, NY 10010
First published in the United States of America in 1988

Printed in Great Britain

ISBN 0-312-02727-3

Library of Congress Cataloging-in-Publication Data

Edwards, Owen Dudley.
    Macaulay/Owen Dudley Edwards.
        p.   cm.—(Historians on historians)
    Bibliography: p.
    Includes index.
    ISBN 0-312-02727-3
    1. Macaulay, Thomas Babington Macaulay, Baron, 1800–1859.
2. Historians—Great Britain—Biography.   3. Historiography—Great
Britain.   4. Great Britain—Historiography.   5. Rome—
Historiography.   I. Title.   II. Series.
DA3.M3E38   1988
941.081'092'4—dc19
[B]   88-27594   CIP

Acknowledgements

My first thanks are due to Thomas Babington Macaulay, without whose encouragement this book would never have been written; and hence to my mother, the late Síle Ni Shúilleabháin, Celtic and folklore scholar, who introduced me to *The Lays of Ancient Rome* when I was six, and to my father, Professor R. Dudley Edwards, the leading scholar of Irish Tudor and Stuart historiography of his time, who responded with so much stimulus to my reading of the *History of England* a decade later. My love and gratitude are also recorded with pleasure to: Professor John A. Watt, the late Professor Frederic C. Lane, the late Professor Sir Herbert Butterfield, Professor Robert B. Patterson, Dr J.R.Highfield, Dr Leslie J. Macfarlane, Dr Doreen J. Milne, the late Professor S.T.Bindoff, the late Dr Marjorie Bindoff, Professor Bernard Bailyn, Professor Kenneth J. Fielding, the late J.T.Gwynn, Dr D.C. Riach, Dr Adam Naylor, Dr Colin Affleck, Professor George Shepperson, Professor V.G.Kiernan, Dr Kenneth J. Fielden, Nicolas Barker, Professor G.F.A.Best, Professor Peter D. Marshall and Michael Foot MP, for helping me to shape my thoughts along the way.

I must also thank Roger Jellinek of the *New York Times* (for his constructive advice when I reviewed John Clive's *Macaulay* for him), Professor John Clive (for stimulating conversations in subsequent years), Dr Conor Cruise O'Brien (especially on Edmund Burke), Professor Andrew Hook (particularly on Macaulay's American reputation), Dr William Ferguson and Dr Michael Lynch (notably on Scottish historical questions), Dr John MacInnes (invaluable on Lewis traditions), Dr Nicholas Phillipson (for seminal ideas on Macaulay's view of his audience), Mr Christopher Fyfe (especially on Zachary Macaulay). Dr T.J.Barron was an admirable guiding hand on India and on the Stephen family. Professor W.W.Robson was an unending source of inspiration on what to investigate and how to go about it. Dr Roger Savage has supported my Macaulay studies in every way from readings of Macaulay to illustrate my lectures to reading of this book in proof.

I am most grateful to Dr Robert Robson, Fellow of Trinity College, Cambridge, for enabling me to study Macaulay's Journal, to the Master and Fellows for permitting my access to it, and to its most helpful Librarians. I am deeply obliged to the Librarians of the British Library, the National Library of Ireland, and the University of South Carolina Library. The Librarian, the Deputy Librarian and the staff of Edinburgh University Library have been endless in their patience and kindness to me. The National Library of Scotland deserves individual expressions of gratitude to every member of the eternally benevolent staffs of the Departments of Printed Books and of Manuscripts; Dr T.I. Rae in particular greatly furthered my quest.

I owe much to Amanda Harting and Peter James of Weidenfeld. Allegra Huston's superb directorial eye removed countless solecisms from the manuscript. Juliet Gardiner has been from start to finish of this book a friend, critic and inspiration of such strength and wisdom that even Macaulay's superlatives would fail him.

My wife, Bonnie Lee Dudley Edwards, my children, Leila, Sara and Michael, and my mother-in-law, Elizabeth Balbirnie Lee, made the book possible by their love and fascinating varieties of response to its themes.

Sir Rupert Hart-Davis trained me in research on literary history, and I only wish this book were worthy of his goodness to me. None could be.

None of the above, with the possible exception of the first-named, bears any responsibility for its inadequacies, the chief of which is that Macaulay is too interesting to receive satisfactory treatment in so short a space.

O.D.E.
University of Edinburgh

My father died on 5 June 1988, while this book was in press. He was greatly looking forward to it, and I wish he had seen it.

Chronology

ix

1 Life

... it is but just to say that our intimate acquaintance
with what he would himself have called the anfractu-
osities of his intellect and of his temper, serves only to
strengthen our conviction that he was both a great and
a good man.

> Macaulay, 'JOHNSON, Samuel',
> *Encyclopaedia Britannica*
> (Edinburgh, 8th edn) XII

Thomas Babington Macaulay was born on 25 October 1800, in
Rothley Temple, Leicestershire, the residence of his father's sister
Jean and her husband, Thomas Babington MP. He was baptized
into the Church of England by his father's brother, the Rev. Aulay
Macaulay, to whom Babington had presented the living of Rothley
in 1796. Macaulay's parents, Zachary Macaulay and Selina Mills,
had been married on 26 August 1799.[1]

It was the male line of paternal ancestry which won principal
attention, in those days, from its inheritor and interested contemporaries. The Macaulay identification with England and its Church
began in Macaulay's father's generation. The family's previous associations had been with the Western Isles of Scotland and the Presbyterian faith: its first language was Gaelic. Macaulay as a historian
drew more on oral evidence and folk-memory than has been stressed,
and it is useful to notice the family tradition which would have
been made known to him. It begins with stories of Isle of Lewis
chieftains and freebooters, feud, treachery, vengeance, hairbreadth
escapes and cunning stratagems. One ancestor, Angus, fell fighting
for the Covenanters against Montrose's troops in the service of
Charles 1, at the Battle of Aultdearn in May 1645. Angus does
not seem to have been much of a religious zealot: he took the field
in allegiance to the Mackenzie Earl of Seaforth, and is supposed
to have done so only to avoid the reproaches of his wife. But his

1

grandsons seem to have been more formidable. One of them, Zachary (Issachar), became Chamberlain of Lewis, cunningly protected the interests of his particular Earl of Seaforth who had strayed into support for the Jacobite cause during the insurrection of 1715, and balanced judicious penmanship in English with remarkable success as a Gaelic poet. This Zachary's first cousin, Aulay, became a Presbyterian minister and seems to have been zealous in the cause of the Protestant succession to the throne. Aulay and his son John, born in 1720 and also minister in the Church of Scotland, were involved in a serious attempt, set on foot by John, to capture Prince Charles Edward Stuart in his flight from Culloden in 1746. Father and son received patronage from the powerful Campbell dukes of Argyll, but their zeal to apprehend the fugitive son of the Catholic claimant to the throne was almost certainly religious. (Aulay was minister in the Isle of Harris then, John in the Isle of Barra.) Had they captured Charles they would have placed the Government of George II in a most undesirable dilemma, since large numbers of Charles's subordinates in insurrection had been ruthlessly executed, and yet all Europe would have been revolted by the logical course of comparable retribution upon their Royal leader. Macaulay as historian would single out the execution of Charles I in 1649 as a blunder, and would stress how clearly the success of the invasion of William III against James II in 1688 depended on James escaping unscathed from England, a circumstance which the zeal of some fishermen momentarily put at grave risk. He would seem to have given some thought to his ancestors' fortunate failure of 1746.[2]

Zachary Macaulay the younger was born in 1768, in the Campbell citadel at Inverary, whither his father, the same Rev. John Macaulay, had now been called to the ministerial charge by the Duke of Argyll. He was thus at least a witness, however uncomprehending, of the demeanour of his father on his return from encounters with Dr Samuel Johnson on his tour of the Highlands and the Hebrides in 1773 in the company of the Lowlander James Boswell. Whether the five-year-old Zachary recalled any sign of his father's discomfiture or of family recollection of it later is unknown: he shared with his son Thomas an astonishing memory, and probably also an early development of intellectual powers. Certainly young Tom Macaulay would have cross-examined his father for anything he did know of the meeting, an occasion on which Johnson, on the evidence of the *Journal* of the tour published by Boswell, was fairly

ferocious when provoked by the Rev. John into argument (on a
subject Boswell only mentioned, if he mentioned it at all, on a piece
of his manuscript now lost – it *could* have been to do with the
Stuarts, for whom Johnson cherished a picturesque affection). Boswell concealed the worst part of it: his unpublished account noted
that when the Rev. John had difficulty in containing himself as the
storm burst around him, Johnson

> challenged him hotly 'Mr Macaulay, Mr Macaulay! Don't you
> know that it is very rude to cry eh! eh! when one is talking?'
> Poor Macaulay had nothing to say for himself. But the truth
> is, that it was a sin of ignorance, or mere rusticity.

John Macaulay was accounted a good preacher, but his Gaelic roots
would have weakened his capacity for any of the conversational
fluency needed to deal with either the one visitor who noisily abused
him or the other who condescendingly pardoned him. In the hearing
of the visitors all was well when the Rev. John returned the following
day: 'Mr Macaulay breakfasted with us, being nothing hurt or dis-
mayed by his last night's correction. Being a man of good sense,
he had a just admiration of Dr Johnson.' The Rev. John's family
may have found his private comments less forgiving; and it is possible that his greatest irritation was turned against the Lowlander
so obviously exhibiting the zoological phenomena of the region
to his great man. Besides, Boswell stood badly with the Duchess,
to whose drawing room in the Castle the Rev. John accompanied
the travellers. Thomas Babington Macaulay in his writings on Johnson and Boswell made no mention of the misfortunes of his grandfather, but in his first essay on Johnson (*Edinburgh Review*,
September 1831), he alluded to Boswell's own account of his ill
success at Inverary Castle ('how impertinent he was to the Duchess
of Argyle and with what stately contempt she put down his imperti-
nence'). The first foundation of Thomas Macaulay's lifelong distaste
for Boswell as a person and delight for him as a biographer may
have been laid at Inverary; and so too may have been the powerful
theme in his *History* of the mutual detestation of Highlander and
Lowlander.[3]

Young Zachary's mother was a Campbell, but he himself had
little reason to thank the clan. His father's last call was to Cardross,
where he lived from 1774 until his death in 1789, and whence

Zachary at sixteen was sent to Jamaica as a plantation bookkeeper. The boy had been told of important introductions to advance his prospects from the former governor, General Sir Archibald Campbell of Inverneil; but he found they proved useless. His own work became that of an overseer, and after five years he returned to Britain with an implacable hatred of slavery which subsequently dominated his whole life, and was fundamental in that of his eldest son. Back in Britain Babington, the husband of an elder sister and friend of an elder brother, provided the comfort of senior wisdom no longer available from Cardross where Zachary's parents died in 1789 and 1790. Zachary had lost his religion: Babington, a devout Evangelical, found him another. The crusade against slavery was thoroughly integrated into this new, exciting, romantic doctrine in which man could play a part in working out his salvation – in contrast to the Calvinism of the Rev. John Macaulay, holding that all things had been settled in advance by divine predestination. The Rev. John had apparently been dismissive of his son's anger against the plantation system which had given him a job. Babington and his Evangelical friends opened up a new orthodoxy of the mind. But Zachary's conviction made him both revolutionary and conservative. Some of the most powerful interests in the England where he would ultimately settle were implacable upholders of slavery, and the Church Establishment was contemptuous of the new zealots who challenged its complacency. Apart from these vital matters, Zachary, Babington and their friends were naturally of a conservative cast of mind, and their future colleague in Evangelical leadership, Hannah More, wrote vehement dialogue to put in the mouths of imaginary English villagers denouncing the French Revolution and declaring its claims of equality to be lies.[4]

In the 1790s Zachary served in Sierra Leone, the settlement for freed slaves established by the Evangelicals: he was its Governor from 1794 to 1799. In the words of the great editor of his son's *Letters*, Thomas Pinney, he 'had to face loneliness, disease, harassment from native tribes and foreign slavers, civil disorder, and all the cares of an administrator who was also judge, policeman, legislator, and preacher to his community'. Its capital was bombarded and laid waste by the French in 1794, presumably because it was administered by British subjects. Both then and at all other times Zachary showed extraordinary strength of mind, a shining example of unflinching readiness to take tough measures for the preservation of freedom. His salutary severity had no truck with dishonesty: he was convinced of the need to be an example in all of his actions so that public morality would be shown as wholly consistent with private. His conviction that rank and leadership must justify themselves and compel respect was increased by his mercifully brief encounter with the French revolutionary navy, where he was disgusted by the want of discipline induced by incessant deference to the symbols of equality. In his work as an administrator he showed that he saw Christianity not only as vital in itself to human salvation, but also as the means by which all men could, if they would, school themselves to become civilized. On his return in 1799 he married Selina Mills, whom he had met on a visit home in 1795.[5]

The young Thomas Babington Macaulay passed his infancy in Birchin Lane, in a house near the Sierra Leone Company, but by 1803 the family had removed to High Street, Clapham, where the presence of many like-minded Evangelicals led to their identification as the 'Clapham Sect'. (The phrase is a little misleading: they remained Anglicans.) The Sect's severity of principle, and Tom's ultimate withdrawal into private religious convictions of which we really know nothing, have led modern writers to see this background as repressive to the point of occasional sadism on his father's part. Certainly Macaulay could exhibit a resentful twinge of reminiscence of his father's severity, when writing in later life in his own journal. But while the two strong minds frequently engaged in superficial conflict, this probably masked a powerful basic harmony. Tom Macaulay's mind opened very early to the acquisition of sophisticated impressions, and it proved very tenacious in clinging to them. Much has been made of his becoming a zealous Whig at Cambridge University and remaining so for the rest of his life, where Zachary had been a stern upholder of Clapham Sect Toryism as the friend of William Wilberforce and an admirer of the younger William Pitt. But Tom Macaulay drew principles and prejudices from his father which he never surrendered to his life's end. His *History* was written in its entirety after his father had died, but it reflects his father's contempt for the High Church, with its sense of God-given right of position independent of the private piety of its individual clerics, and his father's admiration for the moral worth of Evangelicals, whatever their individual absurdities. It has a vigorous contempt for narrow Calvinist theology of the kind his father rejected, but it perpetuates pious Covenanter mythology of the kind his father might be expected to have transmitted. (For instance its portrait of Graham of Claverhouse, afterwards Viscount Dundee, seems the product of nursery tales of a devil-figure, solemnly repeating folklore of Dundee and his men choosing to call themselves by devils' names; in other contexts Macaulay would be the first to scout such nonsense by common-sense reflection which in this case would have noted that such acquaintance with infernal theology was much more in keeping with Covenanter learning than with the festive habits of dragoons.) It extols stern measures in defence of liberty. It is suspicious of hereditary privilege, and quick to show instances where exaltation of noble rank induces habits of idleness and depravity. It is enthusiastic about sound business enterprise (Zachary made a fortune in trade with Africa and the East and West Indies), but it is bitterly hostile to avarice (Zachary's involvement in anti-slavery and consequent inattention to his business left him a ruined man in 1833). It is harsh in isolating deplorable human weaknesses, but it keeps a sharp lookout for redeeming features (Zachary's search for anti-slavery allies led him to speak with respect for persons as little in keeping with his own predilections as Charles James Fox, Lord Byron and Pope Gregory XVI). It takes dark views of the corruption of the world, but it lays great stress on the individual capacities of human beings to prove their moral capabilities. Zachary would not have agreed with all of it; but he would probably have subscribed to a surprising amount.[6]

Macaulay and his father seem to have fascinated one another from the outset, and while there is some indication that the son was sometimes frightened of the father, there is even more to suggest that the father was frightened of the son. The child showed himself a voracious reader, and the stories of his precocious maturity of speech are justly famous: how as a four-year-old he offered his parents' friend Hannah More 'a glass of old spirits' on the precedent of Robinson Crusoe, and how he told Lady Waldegrave, after her servant had spilled hot coffee on his legs and, a little later, she asked if he was any better, 'Thank you, madam, the agony is abated.' Zachary saw that he had fathered an extraordinary fledgling, and worried deeply that he himself would fall short in keeping so fine a mind in tune with its duty to God. Paternal admonition could prove severe; but Zachary, even when Tom was naughty, was far more severe on himself. By the time Tom was thirteen his opinion was being deferentially solicited by his father on the name of the new baby, and he was emphatically and successfully sweeping aside all previous suggestions to pronounce in favour of Charles. Zachary seems to have talked to his eldest son about Scottish heroes such as William Wallace, and Tom enjoyed upholding the virtues of his 'Scotch blood' against his mother and his sister Selina, rejoicing in the evidence of greater Scottish popular support for Christian missionaries being sent to India. Zachary encouraged Tom's enthusiasm for the lays of Sir Walter Scott: the family as a whole went in for reading aloud. Low-church Anglicanism had its doubts about the morality of novels, but this stood little in Tom's way, and at eighteen he was lecturing his father on the folly of his fellow Evangelicals who condemned good and healthy modern literature out of hand. On the other hand, Tom became aware that his father's anti-slavery principles and Scottish origin were often made the occasion for scurrilous attacks, and some of his own most intransigent future vendettas would be against enemies of the anti-slavery cause, such as the dead James Boswell and the living Robert Montgomery. It is true that Zachary's protests resulted in Tom's most reluctantly ceasing to contribute to *Knight's Quarterly Magazine* in 1823, but after the lapse of only one number Zachary gave way: the issue had turned on the supposed impropriety of some of its content, which had included (very) faintly erotic verse and fiction from Tom. Perhaps Tom made amends later in his denunciations of Byronic posing by young men at university, although the same essay, on Moore's *Life* of Byron (*Edinburgh Review*, June 1831), gives strong reason to suppose that Zachary (and maybe Tom too) wept when Byron died at Missalonghi in April 1824.[7]

Tom talked a lot, but he also listened. Future critics would complain that his portrait of the Highlands in his *History* was based on very few sources: what he did not say was that in addition to those formal sources he also owed much to the novels of Scott and to family tradition, on which his father must have been his principal authority (though no doubt something was owed to his aunt Jean, to his uncle Aulay and to the military hero of the family in whose cult his father encouraged him, Zachary's brother General Colin Macaulay who had served in India). Hannah More liked Tom, and he stayed with her during many summers from the age of six: she became one of his earliest sources of oral evidence by supplying information about Johnson, Boswell, David Garrick and other famous figures she had known in her somewhat less straitlaced youth. William Wilberforce supplied Tom with information he would use to great effect later, such as in the Commons debates leading to the impeachment of Warren Hastings. Edmund Burke, vivid in Wilberforce's and Hannah More's memories, became to Macaulay 'the greatest man then living', when he was writing of the late eighteenth century, and his description of Burke in his essay on Hastings (*Edinburgh Review*, October 1841), seems in part a tribute to Zachary, then recently dead:

> Burke was a man in whom compassion for suffering, and hatred of injustice and tyranny, were as strong as in Las Casas or Clarkson. And although in him, as in Las Casas and in Clarkson, these noble feelings were alloyed with the infirmity which belongs to human nature, he is, like them, entitled to this great praise, that he devoted years of intense labour to the service of a people with whom he had neither blood nor language, neither religion nor manners in common, and from whom no requital, no thanks, no applause could be expected.

In that public place he could not mention Zachary's name; but all the same arguments applied to Zachary, and surely his use of the anti-slavery issue indicates that Zachary was in his heart.[8]

Zachary had been forced to grow old very early, and his sense of what was expected in a father would also have been based on a model of considerable seniority, his own father having been forty-eight when he himself was born. But Zachary had found in Babington, ten years his senior, something of a surrogate father, which accounts for his paternal relations with Tom being a mixture of the remote and the collegial. Zachary was also close to his eldest daughter. The younger children – Tom was the first of nine – saw chiefly the remoteness, and here Tom, in his turn, became something of a surrogate father. This was to draw him into a companionship with his sisters Hannah and Margaret, ten and twelve years his juniors respectively. It had a singular effect on his emotional development. He found his fulfilment in writing or talking to them, and he became so dependent on them that their marriages in the early 1830s blasted his life, and Margaret's death soon afterwards came close to costing him his reason and may even have led to serious thoughts of suicide. (At the age of nineteen, in 1831, Margaret had written secretly of him, 'If my dearest, dearest, dearest Tom still loves me, and I am not separated from him, I feel now as if I could bear anything,' in musing about the remote future she was never to have.) He had been able to talk to them with a freedom he did not enjoy either with his father or with his increasingly neurasthenic mother. For one thing, Tom thirsted for praise but was desperately shy of receiving it from outside his family; Zachary worried about praise turning Tom's head, and was unsure of how to respond when praise was called for. So we have the touching, faintly absurd and slightly tragic moment when Tom, aged twenty-three, made a successful anti-slavery speech, and applause surrounded him, and Zachary, clearly but silently bursting with pride, with tears in his eyes when Tom was speaking, murmured some reproof to his son after the meeting about not keeping his arms folded when speaking in the presence of a Royal duke. It was also revelatory of the caution of a Highland Scot, always conscious of involuntarily offending the custom of a strange country.[9]

Tom's education began at home with his parents. At six he was showing familiarity with Virgil, and mastery of elementary Latin composition: Latin and Greek authors were his favourite serious reading all his adult life. He attended a day school in Clapham, but was removed when he was twelve to the Rev. Matthew Preston's boarding school in Cambridgeshire (subsequently transferred to Hertfordshire). He entered Trinity College, Cambridge just before turning eighteen, and seems to have found himself at some social, though not intellectual, disadvantage in the vocal, self-advertising herd of old Etonians. Between 1822 and 1824 he became an orator of power, though not grace, in the Cambridge Union: his contemporary, collaborator and rival Winthrop Mackworth Praed in a verse lampoon of a debate spoke of 'his arms and his metaphors crossed' but termed him, however ironically, 'the favourite'. (Macaulay was always awkward with his hands, save that one of them was an almost tireless writer.) Zachary and Selina had encouraged Tom in infant versifying (his subjects varied from hell to the younger Pitt) and he won the Chancellor's English verse medal twice, as well as an award for a prose essay on William III. He also won the Latin Declamation Prize in 1818, and several scholarships, but took his baccalaureate without honours in 1822 for want of mathematical skills. He tried unsuccessfully for a Trinity Fellowship in 1823 but obtained one in October 1824.

Apart from the one number from which he excluded himself in

deference to Zachary, Tom was a highly successful contributor to all issues of *Knight's Quarterly Magazine*, which made six appearances. It featured the work of a close circle of University literary friends, headed by Praed and by a son and a nephew of the poet Samuel Taylor Coleridge. On his return to *Knight's*, Tom celebrated his accord with his father by composing an amusing couple of scenes supposedly for a play about the origin of Alcibiades' disgrace in the Peloponnesian War, the best portion of which is a dialogue between a censorious father and a conceited artistic son:

CALLIDEMUS. Oh Hercules! This is too much. Here is an universal genius; sophist, – orator, – poet. To what a three-headed monster have I given birth! a perfect Cerberus of intellect! And pray what may your piece be about? Or will your tragedy, like your speech, serve equally for any subject?
...
SPEUSIPPUS. You are sneering. Really, father, you do not understand these things. You had not those advantages in your youth —
CALLIDEMUS. Which I have been fool enough to let you have....

This speaks well for the capacities of both Zachary and Tom to laugh at themselves, and that in their turn gave a sound basis for the comic genius which informed so much of Macaulay's writing all his life. It is also noteworthy that this and so many of Macaulay's other contributions to *Knight's* are primarily light-hearted, and that therefore his first appearance before a portion, however small, of the reading world beyond Cambridge (Charles Knight was a London publisher) was designed to show that scholarly knowledge was fun.[10]

There is a certain element of exhibitionism in these cheerful flourishes of erudition, although there is also a missionary desire to draw his audience into his own extent of learning by showing how much pleasure it can give. *Knight's* also gave Macaulay and his fellows the means of seeking a number of media through which to display their knowledge. Apart from the classical fragments of fiction and drama, Macaulay tried his hand at verse from the standpoint of imaginary bards and witnesses to specific events and movements in history: the Huguenot defeat at Moncontour in 1569, the Huguenot victory at Ivry in 1590, the Cavaliers' March on London in 1642, and the Roundheads' victory at Naseby in 1645. He was showing his mastery of the cultural and ideological materials of history, all within a religious context – this last preoccupation thanks to his parents, indeed doubly thanks to them since Tom's reading aloud the deeply touching 'Moncontour' to his family induced his father to drop his opposition to Tom's further appearances in *Knight's*: Charles Knight learned that all was well from a letter (now lost) enclosing 'Moncontour' and 'Ivry'. The method produced Macaulay's first real successes in giving his reader a sense of being present, especially with 'The Battle of Naseby', producing an almost physical shock as Prince Rupert's troops scatter the Puritans and the narrator is convinced he is about to be killed. (His fictional and dramatic evocations of Caesar and Alcibiades have no such effect: one is simply watching Macaulay observing himself in a state of imagination.) But 'Ivry' operates on two levels: the rejoicings of the Huguenot bard for the Protestant victory culminate in jubilations over the defeat of Catholicism, while the reader knows that all his innocent plaudits for Henry of Navarre ironically reveal the care of Henry, even at the hour of victory, not to alienate the French Catholics whose faith – though his bard does not realize it – he will shortly embrace:

And then we thought of vengeance, and, all along our van,
'Remember St Bartholomew', was passed from man to man.
But out spake gentle Henry, 'No Frenchman is my foe:
Down, down with every foreigner, but let your brethren go.'
Oh! was there ever such a knight, in friendship or in war,
As our Sovereign Lord, King Henry, the soldier of Navarre?[11]

Macaulay's contributions to *Knight's* reflected two preoccupations, both critical of himself and of his country at that moment. The Whig party had been riven asunder by the French Revolution, some following Burke, some Fox, and some, like Sir James Mackintosh, beginning by joining Fox in supporting the Revolution and then finding themselves alongside Burke in opposition to it. The 1820s were showing political tendencies which would bring about a new Whig coalition to arrive in power in 1830. At the same time the Whigs needed to take stock of their own tradition. They were the party which prided itself on its achievement of the Revolution of 1688–89 when the Catholic James 11 had been driven out, the Protestant William 111 and his wife, James's daughter Mary, were

jointly offered the Crown, and the irregularity of the interference
with normal patterns of succession, even straight Protestant succession, was ordained by the Convention which assembled to meet
the crisis. But few Tories were likely to dispute the wisdom of the
Glorious Revolution, even if they differed from Whigs in assessing
precisely where its glory had lain. Indeed its anti-Catholic provisions
had become the hallmark of the High Tories, grimly resolute against
any attempt to permit Catholics to sit in Parliament or receive emancipation from the various other surviving restrictions on their political and economic advancement. Neither their dead leader, the
younger Pitt, nor their great intellectual ally defected from the Whigs,
Edmund Burke, would have agreed. Burke was a lifelong opponent
of anti-Catholic legislation. Pitt left the premiership for three years
in 1801 because he could not break down George III's resistance
to Catholic Emancipation. The High Tories affirmed their allegiance
to the memories of Pitt and Burke in incessant oration, dissertation
and libation, with scarcely a thought of inconsistency. Thereby they
offered an obvious target. But a deeper historiographical debate
was long overdue. It would be simple enough to twit the Tories
with their falseness to the sympathies of Pitt and Burke on Catholic
Emancipation. It was another matter to rally the Whigs to pledges
of Parliamentary Reform and Catholic Emancipation, even at the
cost of Royal opposition of the kind that had driven Pitt from office,
and against whose influence Burke in his younger days had so
strongly declaimed. Such arguments would need to grasp the nettle
of the French Revolution, answer the charge that constitutional
concessions would be the first step on a similar downward path
for the United Kingdom, and assert that it was Tory and Royal
opposition to just reforms which could set revolutionary consequences in motion. To put an anti-Royalism in an English context
was no mere matter of invoking 1688–89, as all sides did. It was
necessary to take up the older cause of Parliament against Charles
I, on which historiography seemed to have had it all Charles's way.
The two greatest historians of modern England, the Royalist Edward
Hyde, first Earl of Clarendon, in the late seventeenth century, and
the Enlightenment philosopher David Hume in the late eighteenth,
had argued that wisdom and justice agreed for Charles at the expense
of his opponents.[12]

Macaulay's views had been swinging towards the Whigs since
his arrival in Cambridge. The conversion was quick, and somewhat

alarming to his parents. Nevertheless Zachary could see that the Tories of the 1820s had reached a pitch of hostility to reform *per se* which boded little good to advocates of anti-slavery in the British Empire (he and his friends had won the abolition of the African Slave Trade in 1807). He had found a vigorous Whig advocate in the writer and orator Henry Brougham, as a result of whose influence Zachary found himself warming to the Whig intellectual Sanhedrin, the *Edinburgh Review*. Zachary could also observe that the supporters of Catholic Emancipation were normally to be relied on to oppose slavery. As to the Whig tradition of enmity to the Stuarts, Zachary could hardly find fault with his son for honouring the traditions variously attested to by his own father and grandfather and their ancestor who had fallen against Charles's soldiers at Aultdearn. Nor would he have wished to leave the last word on any question to David Hume, Lowlander and religious sceptic, and his son had been expressing dissatisfaction with Hume at the age of fourteen. Even on the French Revolution, Zachary's unpleasant memories of the revolutionary French at Sierra Leone had been offset by dislike of the Francophobia which convulsed Britain during the Napoleonic Wars. It was essential to his creed that good men had tried to do their best, however wrong they might have been.

Macaulay while at *Knight's* began with a light-hearted discussion of the quarrel between France and Britain in the 1790s as though it were a dispute between two country parishes, which was amusing in itself – there are engaging verbal caricatures of a whole range of characters from 'Charley the publican' (the bibulous Charles James Fox) to the merry widow 'Mrs Kitty North' (Catherine the Great of Russia) – but its main effect must have been to suggest that the time for letting the Revolution be the bugbear of British politics was over. The same issue had included the Cavalier and Roundhead songs in which, while the savagery of neither side is concealed, the Puritan bard at least has the merit of austere if bigoted high religious principle, while the Cavalier merely sounds like a swaggering bravo exhorting his companions forward with prospect of a few rapes of enticingly puritan maidens. ('The Battle of Naseby' is inspiring, for all of Macaulay's making his brave bard fairly repulsive in the vengeful moment of victory, after his exhibition of heroism when defeat and death had seemed so imminent: Edmund Wilson in *Patriotic Gore* argues that it inspired Julia Ward Howe to write 'The Battle Hymn of the Republic', which in its turn inspired the Northern armies of the American Civil War when that was transformed from a merely constitutional conflict into a crusade to emancipate the slaves. Macaulay had intended that the crusading conviction of his bard would testify to the transformation of anti-Royalist arms from constitutional to social.) The next number of *Knight's* offered a very different apologist for the Puritan cause: Macaulay imagined an observer's account of a friendly argument about the Civil War between the Royalist poet Abraham Cowley and the aged John Milton, set after the Restoration. Its spirit is one of celebration of the cultural richness of the English past, however divided in loyalties, and Cowley is presented as a very sweet person, solicitous in making no pastoral reference which might be hurtful to Milton because of his blindness; but Milton has far the better of the argument.[13]

The oldest and perhaps the most eccentric of Macaulay's Cambridge colleagues on *Knight's* was William Sidney Walker, a Fellow of Trinity by now immersed in preparing for press a newly discovered Latin essay by Milton; Walker was in fact only hired for some literary hackwork in connection with it, but his enthusiasm overshot all bounds, and it became the whole business of his life. It was published in 1825. Macaulay had written his first article for the *Edinburgh Review* on 'West Indian Slavery' just after *Knight's* made its last appearance in November 1824: it appeared in January 1825. Walker's obsession alerted him to the opportunity of his life. Macaulay's own obscure situation (he had by now left Cambridge) placed him in no position to dispute with the giants of the *Edinburgh Review* as to who would be the favoured critic chosen to review fashionable books of the day: Brougham was at the time his supporter, but would become fiendishly jealous later, and the other leading lights such as Sydney Smith, Henry Cockburn and the editor himself, Francis Jeffrey, were also his seniors by twenty years and more. But who was going to gainsay his right to discuss Milton's *De Doctrina Christiana*? He duly discussed it, for the issue of August 1825, in six brief paragraphs, moving on to what was virtually an expository hymn in praise of Milton, whence he came to a defence of Cromwell, of the Puritans, and above all of the ideal of freedom. His name was made.[14]

Macaulay was to write with enormous success for the *Edinburgh* for the next twenty years, and to become a great pundit on historical, literary, social and economic questions. He never short-changed his readers by reliance on his reputation, and his last essay for them (his second on Chatham) was among the best he ever wrote. The essays must be reserved for our discussion of his work. But his 'Milton' was a great event in his life. His style, with its wonderful powers of vivid metaphor and intimate persuasion, was recognized as unique, and his work thereafter would be eagerly looked for by a rapidly widening circle of admirers. People knew him from it: occasionally they ascribed the work of others to him, but for all of the *Edinburgh*'s anonymity and Macaulay's punctilious (if occasionally playful) use of its convention of self-description by the editorial 'we', he might as well have signed his contributions. Jeffrey said he had never seen anything like it, but in fact it attested to the strength of Zachary's tutelage in the Authorised Version of the Bible, with its short and forceful sentences, quick, cumulative and sometimes crushing argument, affection for simile, metaphor and parable. Macaulay's love of literature and delight in ranging through history engaged readers to follow him in search of the one, and contemplate the lessons he deduced from his pageant of the other. His style did change: in publishing his *Critical and Historical Essays* selected from the pages of the *Edinburgh Review* Macaulay would write in 1843:

> the criticism on Milton, which was written when the author was fresh from college, and which contains scarcely a paragraph such as his matured judgment approves, still remains overloaded with gaudy and ungraceful ornament.

But in meeting the expectations of his audience, and indeed of his editors, Macaulay was himself altered by his essay on Milton. In particular, because of his success in reclaiming the historical battleground where the Tories had been in high command, he was widely regarded as the Whig advocate from history: in the end his history was to prove far less Whiggish than contemporaries and posterity were to imagine, but he was summoned to its deployment in the Whig cause, and hence Whig journalism may be said to have made him a historian. The Whigs had had Burke as an advocate from history; but the French Revolution had taken him and his legacy to the enemy camp, although Macaulay would strive with his utmost to regain that legacy. Fox had tried his hand with history; he left only a fragment. Mackintosh was working on a history of the Revolution of 1688, but his antiquarian benevolence made him no match for the embattled John Wilson Croker of the *Quarterly Review*, and certainly not for the dead Tory giants Clarendon and Hume. Macaulay was to become the great popular historian, and he became it almost by popular demand.[15]

In part he owed the success of 'Milton' to its unabashed romanticism. His father, even in his theology, was a romantic; his friends on *Knight's* had been too, as one might expect from the son and nephew of Coleridge. Jeffrey and his associates had offered the hard-hitting rationality of the Enlightenment, most crushingly asserted in Jeffrey's own review of Wordsworth's *Excursion* which began 'This will never do'; within a few years of his 'Milton' Macaulay was writing in the *Edinburgh* of 'the reverence we feel for the genius of Mr Wordsworth'. The 'Milton' essay explicitly tied his romanticism to his great sense of involvement with the giants of the past, although it did so with much more exposure of machinery than he would afterwards employ. In any case, it was a romanticism his audience wanted to hear, and a summons to which it wished to respond:

> We are transported a hundred and fifty years back. We can almost fancy that we are visiting him in his small lodging; that we see him sitting at the old organ beneath the faded green hangings; that we can catch the quick twinkle of his eyes, rolling in vain to find the day; that we are reading in the lines of his noble countenance the proud and mournful history of his glory and his affliction. We image to ourselves the breathless silence in which we should listen to his slightest word, the passionate veneration with which we should kneel to kiss his hand and weep upon it....
>
> These are perhaps foolish feelings. Yet we cannot be ashamed of them; nor shall we be sorry if what we have written shall in any degree excite them in other minds.

He grasped the nettle of the execution of the King, deplored it but defended its authors and relentlessly twitted the Tory upholders of the Revolution of 1688–89 with inconsistency:

> What essential distinction can be drawn between the execution of the father and the deposition of the son? What constitutional

maxim is there which applies to the former and not to the latter? The King can do no wrong. If so, James was as innocent as Charles could have been. The minister only ought to be responsible for the acts of the Sovereign. If so, why not impeach Jeffreys and retain James? The person of a King is sacred. Was the person of James considered sacred at the Boyne? To discharge cannon against an army in which a King is known to be posted is to approach pretty near to regicide.[16]

Above all, he offered an answer to the plea that the cause of liberty meant horrors such as the French Revolution: 'There is only one cure for the evils which newly acquired freedom produces; and that cure is freedom.'[17]

His next essay for the *Edinburgh*, on the newly founded London University (of which his father was secretary of the board of trustees) asserted the old Scottish principle of the right to education for the widest possible number. This would be a principle of his writing career, in that he saw his own work as a means of advancing that universal education. He began, soon after, to contemplate a history of England under the Stuarts for the Society for the Diffusion of Useful Knowledge, a body consecrated to such an ideal and served, among others, by Thomas Flower Ellis, who was to become his closest lifelong friend. Meanwhile, in prose and verse, he was giving of his best to the struggle for Catholic Emancipation. With the retirement of Lord Liverpool, the Government under George Canning was losing the support of the High Tories and gaining that of the Whigs. Macaulay wrote passionately for the *Edinburgh* in its favour, and warned the High Tories that if they continued to stand in the way of popular demands they might share the fate of the aristocrats exiled by the French Revolution (he stopped short of threatening them with the guillotine). He was appointed a Commissioner of Bankrupts, which was a valuable financial support; he was a barrister now, but briefs were slow in coming his way. In February 1830 he was elected MP for Calne on the sponsorship of the Marquess of Lansdowne, who controlled the borough. Catholic Emancipation had been achieved the previous year, despite the disasters of Canning's death and the disintegration of his coalition, and so Macaulay's maiden speech was against the civil disabilities still oppressing Jews.[18]

The four years that followed caught him up in extraordinary

excitement. He was fascinated by the Revolution of 1830 in France which ousted the restored Bourbons, this time for ever, and he wrote part of a draft of a book on French history beginning at their Restoration in 1814. But the pressure of Parliamentary events and his work for the *Edinburgh* led him to abandon it. His research supplied notes of grim warning against his Tory opponents during the Parliamentary Reform Bill debates, in which he quickly became known as one of the greatest speakers on the Whig side. In point of historical reference his leading opponent was John Wilson Croker, who further enraged him by taking up Winthrop Mackworth Praed, now shorn of his former Whig principles to become a factious Tory spokesman against Reform: Macaulay took his warfare into literary criticism and did terrible execution on Croker's edition of Boswell's *Johnson*:

> We are sorry to be obliged to say that the merits of Mr Croker's performance are on a par with those of a certain leg of mutton on which Dr Johnson dined, while travelling from London to Oxford, and which he, with characteristic energy, pronounced to be 'as bad as bad could be; ill fed, ill killed, ill kept, and ill dressed'. This edition is ill compiled, ill arranged, ill written, and ill printed.

(He went on, after ruthless disputation of error after error in Croker's notes, to dissect Boswell as a virtually worthless man and wholly peerless biographer, and to present Johnson almost as vividly as he appears in the book Macaulay loved so well.)[19]

Macaulay had been in the House of Commons for over a year when he made his first visit to Holland House, ruled with a rod of iron (and a fairly painful fan) by Lady Holland, wife of the nephew of Charles James Fox. (Lord Holland had accepted Cabinet office in the Whig government under Charles Earl Grey which had replaced Wellington's Tory administration in 1830.) Macaulay quickly became a favourite at Holland House, and while he talked, as usual, a great deal, and quickly became an instant point of reference for almost any historical fact in dispute, (and from time to time was instructed by her Ladyship that that was enough of that subject), he drew out the gouty old Lord on his memories of the past and particularly on the career and reminiscences of his illustrious uncle. But for all of the patronage of the Hollands, his own fine orations in the Commons, and his unrivalled popularity in the *Edinburgh*, Macaulay never quite obtained acceptance from the Whig leadership. For all his pride in England, there seemed something unEnglish about his loquacity, his almost sensual love of learning, his voracious enthusiasm for curious folksongs and obscure plays and pamphlets. Calne would be reduced to one MP under the Reform Act of 1832, and the MP would be Lansdowne's son; and when Macaulay therefore went forward (successfully) for election at Leeds in late 1832, a local supporter noted in his diary that the candidate was 'Mr Mackholy the Scotchman'. Macaulay's enthusiasm for the past could be an irritant to the Whig leaders; thus in his gorgeous account of the opening in 1788 of the trial of Warren Hastings before the House of Lords (*Edinburgh Review*, October 1841) he includes an admiring description of the young Grey almost immediately after a rapturous glimpse of Georgiana, Duchess of Devonshire, who had then been Grey's mistress and shortly afterwards bore his illegitimate child: a mistress of Grey's successor, Lord Melbourne, receives incidental mention. In neither case, of course, was the lady's association with the nobleman mentioned, and Macaulay may have known nothing of Grey's amours – Zachary's son would hardly have written of his 'unblemished honour' with such knowledge – but one cannot think of either premier reading the account with much satisfaction. Macaulay's origins were, by Whig aristocratic standards, low (if not by those of Lady Holland, a Jamaican divorcee), and his support for his father's antislavery beliefs made him conspicuously ready to oppose the Whig government when it wanted to soft-pedal the demand for the abolition of slavery throughout the Empire. His financial situation required him to be a placehunter; the abolition of his Commissionership of Bankrupts in 1832 made him dependent on Whig charity for a place, and while he was made a member of the Board of Control later the same year, Grey conspicuously refrained from marking his invaluable oratorical services with a seat in the Cabinet. Eventually, in late 1833, he was forced by the worsening economic circumstances of his family to accept membership of the Supreme Council of India, with departure the following year and consequent resignation from his seat in Parliament.[20]

For all of these disappointments, he luxuriated in the Commons battles over the Whig measures for Reform of Parliament, quickening the fascination of an ordinary viewer with his sense of being present at an event comparable to some of the greatest moments in the history of the Chamber of which he was now a member. His work for the *Edinburgh* on seventeenth- and eighteenth-century subjects kept its past perpetually before his eyes. His letters to his young sisters were written simultaneously to give the highest degree of entertainment and to convey a description as he himself would love to have found it, and occasionally did find it, in the published correspondence of the dead. Swift's *Journal to Stella* is an obvious parallel and one which Macaulay himself would have had very much in mind. Some of his letters to Ellis at this time bear the same character, if not tone; such as that of 30 March 1831 recording the Commons division on the first Reform Bill when the Grey administration had feared it would be defeated:

> But you might have heard a pin drop as Duncannon read the numbers. Then again the shouts broke out – and many of us shed tears – I could scarcely refrain. And the jaw of Peel fell; and the face of Twiss was as the face of a damned soul; and Herries looked like Judas taking his neck-cloth off for the last operation.

(Herries had brought down the Canningite government under Lord Goderich by leaving it in 1828 and then taken office under Wellington; Macaulay in some verses had declared that his name stank like the main London sewer, so the analogy had some preparation.)[21]

Recent historiography has argued that the Reform Act, far from being a revolution, prolonged the power of the landed aristocracy and gentry which had consolidated its hegemony following the events of 1688–89. But Macaulay believed it was a bloodless revolution, which had averted a bloody one. Its events had been attended by some bloodshed: Bristol fell into the hands of a mob in October 1831 and part of it was set on fire. King William IV, unlike his brother George IV whom he had succeeded in 1830, went along with Grey's administration in the initial moves for Reform, but grew fearful, sought unsuccessfully to bring back the Tories when opposition in the Lords defeated the first Reform Bill, and caused Macaulay, writing to Hannah and Margaret, to fear he 'had entered on the path of Charles [I] and Louis [XVI]', both of whom were executed by their subjects. The tangible result of the Reform Act in his own case was a powerful symbol. He had sat in Parliament for Calne, where he was absolutely dependent on an aristocratic patron, although in practice he truckled to him little enough, too little for Lord Lansdowne's liking. Had his presence not been so indispensable to the Whigs, the cautious patron and the headstrong politician might have fallen out; as it was, the passing doubts were forgotten, Macaulay gratefully dedicated his *Speeches* to Lansdowne twenty years later, and all that survives in his published writings to show his restiveness at such curbs on his Parliamentary integrity are his attacks on the patronage system in literature. He evidently saw the Reform Act as doing for politics what time had done for literature, subjecting men of talent to the judgment of the educated public instead of to the whims of a capricious patron. His new constituency at Leeds had been enfranchised by the Act, and during 1833 he sat in Parliament as a symbol that the rising significance of British industrial capitalists and the towns in which they operated could no longer be excluded from recognition. He believed himself to have been witness and participant in the concluding process of a constitutional revolution inaugurated by the Revolution of 1688–89, and prefigured by the Civil War and Commonwealth of 1641–60.[22]

He certainly did not believe in the extension of the franchise beyond the elements of society given the vote in 1832. As he saw it, power should only be given to the educated. But as he strove for the furtherance of education as widely as possible his thought must be taken as presuming appropriate extension of political power in the fullness of time. He assumed that education would put economic advancement into the hands of those who sought and obtained it. His inheritance of hostility to slavery led to his opposition to any barriers against advancement induced by considerations of race, religion or previous condition of servitude, and he was not hostile to ultimate enfranchisement of educated women. He declared that no objection could be made to marriage between black and white persons save that which economic divisions might induce, and with education and economic opportunities these would disappear (*Edinburgh Review*, March 1827). His identification with the successful struggle of the Catholics, and with the much longer deferred emancipation of the Jews, was based on the same reasoning. He thought of his fight for Reform in 1831–32 as a real crusade of Progress against Bigotry because the most notable of his opponents had been conspicuously anti-Catholic in 1827–28; Wellington's leading supporters only became (very reluctant) converts to Catholic Emancipation in 1829 under the duress of Daniel O'Connell's mammoth agitation in Ireland. On the other hand, knowing of the traditions of popular Protestantism, he could judge how the anti-Catholic masses in England would have prevented Catholic Emancipation if they had the power, and his second campaign for Jewish Emancipation, that in 1833, was in part a reply not only to the Tory bigots but also to new tribunes of popular sentiment such as William Cobbett. Macaulay's implacable hostility to racial and religious barriers in public life – and he saw both of them as essentially the result of the same prejudices – derived from his own consciousness of being the child of a racially mixed marriage. He always spoke of the Celt as racially separate from the Saxon, and he well knew his paternal ancestors to be Celts in language, society and culture, however Protestant. He avoided Scottish subjects in his writing for the *Edinburgh* in the 1830s (apart from Boswell), being courageous but not foolhardy. His 'Milton' had begun with a learned little joke to the effect that Milton's Protestant theological concerns expressed in a treatise in Latin 'compelled him to use many words/ "That would have made Quintilian stare and gasp"' – he assumed his *Edinburgh* readers would know that it was Scottish names Milton had declared would inspire the putative staring and gasping he so inescapably identified with the innocent Quintilian. This was so delicate as to be almost invisible, but it shows a sensitivity to Scotophobia even from lips as hallowed as Milton's. It was not until his last essay for the *Edinburgh* (October 1844) that he exhibited his full sense of the racial hostilities against which his father had struggled so long and which he may have realized were more powerful against himself than he cared to acknowledge. His context is the sudden rise of Lord Bute on the accession of his pupil George III in 1760:

> The two sections of the great British people had not yet been indissolubly blended together. The events of 1715 and of 1745 had left painful and enduring traces. The tradesmen of Cornhill had been in dread of seeing their tills and warehouses plundered by barelegged mountaineers from the Grampians. They still recollected that Black Friday, when the news came that the rebels were at Derby, when all the shops in the city were closed, and when the Bank of England began to pay in sixpences. The Scots,

on the other hand, remembered with natural resentment, the
severity with which the insurgents had been chastised, the military
outrages, the humiliating laws, the heads fixed on Temple Bar,
the fires and quartering blocks on Kennington Common. The
favourite did not suffer the English to forget from what part
of the island he came. The cry of all the south was that the
public offices, the army, the navy, were filled with high-cheeked
Drummonds and Erskines, Macdonalds and Macgillivrays, who
could not talk a Christian tongue, and some of whom had but
lately begun to wear Christian breeches. All the old jokes on
hills without trees, girls without stockings, men eating the food
of horses, pails emptied from the fourteenth storey, were pointed
against these lucky adventurers. To the honour of the Scots it
must be said, that their prudence and their pride restrained them
from retaliation. Like the princess in the Arabian tale, they
stopped their ears tight, and, unmoved by the shrillest notes of
abuse, walked on, without once looking round, straight towards
the Golden Fountain.

We don't know if Macaulay's name induced a revival of 'All the
old jokes' when he was at school and at Cambridge, but neither
institution is likely to have been frugal with them.[23]

This identification of his own racial situation with others partly
or wholly beyond the Saxon pale, and its assumption that the
desideratum was complete integration of all English subjects within
the British state, was to dominate his work in India. While still
in the Commons, on 10 July 1833 he had concluded a speech on
the government of India:

It may be that the public mind of India may expand under our
system till it has outgrown that system; that by good government
we may educate our subjects into a capacity for better government; that, having become instructed in European institutions,
they may, in some future age, demand European institutions....
such a day ... whenever it comes ... will be the proudest day
in English history. To have found a great people sunk in the
lowest depths of slavery and superstition, to have so ruled them
as to have made them desirous and capable of all the privileges
of citizens, would indeed be a title to glory all our own.

23

This he saw as a much surer victory than that brought by mere dependence on force of arms:

> there are triumphs which are followed by no reverse. There is an empire exempt from all natural causes of decay. These triumphs are the pacific triumphs of reason over barbarism; that empire is the imperishable empire of our arts and our morals, our literature and our laws.

It was cultural imperialism, but, however much the citation might have annoyed him, it was what David Hume had undertaken to do in teaching the English; and it was what his father had also done in seeking to impose his moral principles on the English. Much has been made of the fact that Macaulay's mission to India followed Utilitarian teaching. He had castigated James Mill's views on representative government, which he found excessively democratic and chimerical. He came to admire Mill when he read his *History of British India*, probably in January 1832. He was deeply touched when he learned that Mill had used his influence in his favour in 1833 to gain him his Indian post. His Indian career certainly harmonized admirably with Utilitarian views as to the protection and education of the Indians. But in certain respects his achievement is attributable less to the influence of Mill, with whose view of Indian history he maintained some disagreement, than to that of his childhood reading of Daniel Defoe. Robinson Crusoe would teach Man Friday English; he did not invite much comparable instruction in Friday's language and culture, where this was not of immediate practical use. Macaulay's father had seen it as his duty to bring order and civilization to Sierra Leone. Macaulay wrote from India to Zachary (whom he was never to see alive again) on 12 October 1836 in language which made very clear their continuing common purposes:

> We have got rid of the punishment of death except in cases of aggravated treason and wilful murder. We shall also get rid indirectly of everything that can properly be called slavery in India . . . no person will be entitled, on the plea of being the master of another, to do anything to that other which it would be an offence to do to a freeman.

He was alluding to the Indian penal code, which he had been drafting very much on the principle that Indian subjects should have full legal protection and should win ultimate full citizenship once education and prosperity made them eligible for it. Here he was particularly fortified by the support he had received from Lord William Bentinck, the Governor-General in office when he arrived in June 1834 and whom in spite of their overlap lasting but nine months Macaulay (according to Hannah) regarded subsequently as 'the greatest man he had ever known'. Macaulay played a vital part in the extension of freedom of the press to India, and in curbing the special privileges enjoyed by British residents under the law in contrast to the legal limits placed on Indians. These changes went into operation, though they induced widespread indignation among the British-born in India. The penal code had to wait twenty years to be adopted, and was then put into practice only in part. Macaulay's principle was that all possible barriers in the way of recognition of racial equality be removed. This included his famous argument in the Minute on Indian Education, calling for absolute priority for cultural Anglicization of India. He had virtually no sympathy with the position of persons interested in Indian culture and antiquities, whose furtherance he saw as likely to maintain the obstacles in the way of Indian advancement. If he had lost common ground with his father in formal adherence to the Evangelical faith, he still regarded it as a necessary requirement in human advancement. He continued in his letter to Zachary:

No Hindoo who has received an English education ever continues to be sincerely attached to his religion. Some continue to profess it as a matter of policy. But many profess themselves pure Deists, and some embrace Christianity. The case with Mahometans is very different. The best educated Mahometan often continues to be a Mahometan still. The reason is plain. The Hindoo religion is so extravagantly absurd that it is impossible to teach a boy astronomy, geography, natural history, without completely destroying the hold which that religion has on his mind. But the Mahometan religion belongs to a better family. It has very much in common with Christianity; and even where it is most absurd, it is reasonable when compared with Hindooism.

In 1843, when he had once more obtained a seat in Parliament and the Tories had returned to power, he attacked the Tory Governor-

General Lord Ellenborough in the severest terms for having lent his official support to the restoration of the gates of a temple to the deity Shiva the Destroyer, at Somnauth.[24]

Ironically, at the very point in his Indian years when he was so vigorously supporting Lord William's policy of Anglicization, his private study lay in imagining the possible character of a culture completely lost, the Latin ballads once widely sung and subsequently forgotten, songs of heroic moments in mythological Roman history; he carried this work to fruition in 1842 with the publication of his *Lays of Ancient Rome*. His justification would be that nobody was now in danger of having his progress retarded by cults of Janus or Jupiter, the Roman Tiber or the Roman wolf. In part it may have been psychological compensation for the rigour with which he set his face against Indian antiquities. He believed in progress but saw it as essentially inimical to poetry, which he regarded as the product of a simple and natural world finding its greatest human expression in his adored Homer, who he remarked in an article written during his first months in India 'probably did not know a letter' (*Edinburgh Review*, June 1835). But he would not run the risk of giving a new lease of life to barriers against Indian advancement by conceding that India might have its Homers too. Indeed, he believed the material progress in any part of India where his Minute on Education would apply must make such a thing impossible. Pure Indian society, whatever its merits – and he acknowledged very few – had been destroyed with the advance of British power.[25]

Still, Macaulay needed that early work on what would ultimately be his 'Horatius'. His Indian residence coincided with the greatest blow of his life. He had written his sister Margaret ten letters from India, mostly very long, the last of them on Christmas Eve 1834. But she never saw them. Early in January 1835 he received news that she had died of scarlet fever on 12 August. Although her marriage had caused him great pain, it was nothing to this. His tragically one-sided correspondence shows how powerful his emotional dependence on her remained, all the more as Hannah, who had gone out to India with him, had promptly fallen in love with, and married, the administrator Charles Trevelyan. Henceforth Macaulay was a man with a psychological wound which never healed. Fifteen years later he could still be reduced to cruel, helpless weeping by seeing a picture in Lichfield Cathedral which he had last examined in her company. Hannah and Margaret had been his foremost and first audience. He continued to read his writing, when he resumed it, to Hannah and Trevelyan (counting himself successful when the latter did not go to sleep), but after India, although he may no longer have held any firm faith in life after death, his writing still seems couched for a female audience as like Margaret as he could hope, and, after her, for his memory of Zachary: it was to entertain and inform first, and edify second. Another Margaret did come into his life, though on very different terms: little 'Baba', the eldest child born to Hannah and Trevelyan, became Macaulay's one tangible link with posterity. But she was not a substitute for her namesake; she gave him a joy which could coexist with his eternal grief, but never supplant it. Sometimes the two Margarets supplemented one another: his Roman lay 'Virginia' may be initially founded on the little child, but as the poem proceeds it is clear that the older Margaret is in mind.[26]

Macaulay had always been a great reader, but now only a truly mixed simile will do justice to his condition: after Margaret's death, he read like a drowning man. 'Literature has saved my life and my reason,' he wrote to Ellis on 20 December 1835, almost a year after hearing of it. 'Even now I dare not, in the intervals of business, remain alone for a minute without a book in my hand.' He threw himself thoroughly into Indian business, but his own writing, apart from 'Horatius' and its attendant speculations on early Roman public opinion as filtered much later through subsequent writers, disappeared from his life for almost two years. And his writing had changed. He had produced twenty-seven articles for the *Edinburgh* within ten years; he would write but twelve more, ending in 1844. He would henceforth be more magisterial, more ready to short-cut critical as opposed to expository material, more elegaic and profound in tone. Apart from a hard-hitting but firmly courteous discussion of Gladstone on Church and state (*Edinburgh Review*, April 1839), he avoided purely controversial or topical articles which hitherto had amounted to one-third of his output for the *Edinburgh*. What he wanted now was the past, whether in history or literature. He was to be accused incessantly in times to come of writing history with one eye firmly on the present; whatever the merits of this thesis – and they are mixed – his hunger for history was caused by a necessity to get away from the present. Descartes spoke of history as escapism: it became so, in the chief reason for pursuing it, for Macaulay. If he did not, as austere historians have preached, study the past for its own sake, he did so for his. We can put it most simply by saying that before his Indian journey Macaulay wrote history as a secondary activity to the living of his life in the present; after his return, he saw his life in the present as increasingly secondary to his pursuit of the past. He himself might have compared the situation to that of an hourglass: for the future, his harvest from history to be given to the public grew ever greater, richer, deeper, in proportion as the thread of his life in the present trickled thin and small. In terms of physical health he was an old man in his fifties, and he did not survive them. If suffering is necessary for great art, Macaulay qualifies: grief walked beside him to the end of his days.[27]

When he broke his literary silence in late 1836 it was with an enormous article for the *Edinburgh* (July 1837) on Bacon, of which the opening, introduced on the pretext of biographers' understandable partiality for their subjects, becomes a statement of creed and practice for the historian of culture. It is well to note that he begins cheerfully enough, with that comic sense which never left him:

> The genius of Sallust is still with us. But the Numidians whom he plundered, and the unfortunate husbands who caught him in their houses at unseasonable hours, are forgotten. We suffer ourselves to be delighted by the keenness of Clarendon's observation, and by the sober majesty of his style, till we forget the oppressor and the bigot in the historian. Falstaff and Tom Jones have survived the gamekeepers whom Shakspeare cudgelled and the landladies whom Fielding bilked. A great writer is the friend and benefactor of his readers, and they cannot but judge of him under the deluding influence of friendship and gratitude.

But his own obligations rose above his analysis of the causes of bias in literary biography, as he spoke of

> the feeling which a man of liberal education naturally entertains towards the great minds of former ages. The debt which he owes to them is incalculable. They have guided him to truth. They have filled his mind with noble and graceful images. They have stood by him in all vicissitudes, comforters in sorrow, nurses in sickness, companions in solitude. These friendships are

exposed to no danger from the occurrences by which other attach-
ments are weakened or dissolved. Time glides on; fortune is
inconstant; tempers are soured; bonds which seemed indissol-
uble are daily sundered by interest, by emulation, or by caprice.
But no such cause can affect the silent converse which we hold
with the highest of human intellects. That placid intercourse is
disturbed by no jealousies or resentments. These are the old
friends who are never seen with new faces, who are the same
in wealth and in poverty, in glory and in obscurity. With the
dead there is no rivalry. In the dead there is no change. Plato
is never sullen. Cervantes is never petulant. Demosthenes never
comes unseasonably. Dante never stays too long. No difference
of political opinion can alienate Cicero. No heresy can excite
the horror of Bossuet.[28]

To find anything comparable to this recognition of creativity as
the means of reply to devastating personal deprivation, we have
to turn to Milton's hymn to Light contemplated from his blindness
which begins the Third Book of *Paradise Lost*.

Zachary did not die until 13 May 1838, when Macaulay and
the Trevelyans were nearing England on their return from India.
Here the loss, though great, was not the same darkening of the
future that Margaret's had been; Macaulay had hammered out his
ideas in the past in response to Zachary, and his particular style
of cumulative persuasion derived from his anxiety to supply arguments which would satisfy that severe and affectionate critic, but
that work had been done. Macaulay's prose, especially in the *History*, still has the air of making a case to convince a beloved and
formidable companion, but insofar as he is still talking to Zachary
it is the Zachary of his youth. An audience and critic for future
work was at hand in Ellis, shrewd and sensible in comment, sympathetic to the point of self-abnegation in appreciation. In March
1839 their mutual links were strengthened by common grief, when
Ellis lost first his infant daughter Margaret and then his wife. During
that terrible week of her death, Macaulay's journal, started some
months before, lost its length of daily entry and became nothing
but a terse chronicle of daily visits with only the briefest of words
on Ellis's misery. To Hannah on 20 March he was more detailed,
grimly noting the emptiness of the hope of material glory for them
both:

Poor fellow – he prayed bitterly to God to take him too.... 'Yet' he said 'I was so proud of her. I loved so much to show her to anybody that I valued. And now what good will it do me to be a Judge or to make ten thousand a year? I shall not have her to go home to with the good news.' I could not speak, for I know what that feeling is as well as he.... He ought, he said, to be very grateful that I had not died in India, but was at home to comfort him. Comfort him I could not, except by hearing him talk of her with tears in my eyes.[29]

Apart from Hannah, Macaulay's surviving family meant much less to him. His mother, whose importance in his life seems largely to have diminished between his psychological involvement with his father and his devotion to his youngest sisters, had died with no violent sense of loss to him in 1831; his sister Jean's death in 1830 had hit him harder, but Hannah and Margaret enabled him to recover. In 1838 he had moved in with his sisters Selina and Fanny, and kept pleasant but light associations with his brothers John, Henry and Charles. He could hardly bring himself at first to maintain links with Margaret's husband Edward Cropper, but he seems to have had a good way of conversing with her son, if even more opinionated than with his normal readers. Shakespeare, he assured eight-year-old Charles Cropper on 20 June 1842, was worth Plato, Socrates, Euclid and Archimedes together,

> and so was Homer. When you are able to read Plato and Homer in the Greek, which you will be, I hope, in a few years, you will say just as I say.
> As to Mentor he was an old ass who ought to have had a fool's cap on his head for advising Idomeneus to make such a set of foolish laws.

He also knew how to show love to a child, as on 27 July 1843: 'I shall miss you to day very much ... we should all think the day much more pleasant if we could have you with us.' His heart did go out to Cropper when little Charley died at thirteen. 'I had left the dear boy my library,' he told Ellis on 17 April 1847, 'little expecting that I should ever wear mourning for him.'[30]

Macaulay's return to England in June 1838 enabled him to take advantage of a period of mourning for his father and live very quietly. He resumed work for the *Edinburgh*, for which his massive essay on Bacon had been the sole production of his Indian years after he learned of Margaret's death. The first new essay, on the seventeenth-century diplomat and dilettante Sir William Temple (*Edinburgh Review*, October 1838), showed how close his literary creativity kept to his memory of Margaret, in the trumpet-call for social history arising from his reading of the letters written to Temple by his future wife. Margaret's death had robbed him of such a beloved correspondent, and his account of Dorothy Osborne, afterwards Lady Temple, is exceptionally tender. He was jocular about his fondness for her, which he shared with the author of the work under review:

> Mr Courtenay proclaims that he is one of Dorothy Osborne's devoted servants, and expresses a hope that the publication of her letters will add to the number. We must declare ourselves his rivals. She really seems to have been a very charming young woman, modest, generous, affectionate, intelligent, and sprightly....

The portrait that follows is Dorothy, not Margaret, but its appreciation begins from the same origin. (Something of the same antecedent would be true of his approach to the character of Queen Mary II in the *History*.) Macaulay's writing for the *Edinburgh* reflected more inspiration from private experience, now, where previously its personal quality had naturally arisen from public issues with which he was conspicuously identified. His critique of the then High Tory Gladstone's book on the duties of a state to implement the needs of the Established Church (*Edinburgh Review*, April 1839) contained this example as perhaps its strongest thrust against the injustice of Gladstone's system:

> Here is a poor fellow, enlisted in Clare or Kerry, sent over fifteen thousand miles of sea, quartered in a depressing and pestilential climate. He fights for the Government; he conquers for it; he is wounded; he is laid on his pallet, withering away with fever, under that terrible sun, without a friend near him. He pines for the consolations of that religion which, neglected perhaps in the season of health and vigour, now comes back to his mind, associated with all the overpowering recollections of his earlier days, and of the home which he is never to see again. And because

the state for which he dies sends a priest of his own faith to stand at his bedside, to tell him, in language which at once commands his love and confidence, of the common Father, of the common Redeemer, of the common hope of immortality, because the state for which he dies does not abandon him in his last moments to the care of heathen attendants, or employ a chaplain of a different creed to vex his departing spirit with a controversy about the Council of Trent, Mr Gladstone finds that India presents 'a melancholy picture', and that there is 'a large allowance of false principle' in the system pursued there.

The transformation of Gladstone's proposition into its human terms was based on a mythical example of an individual soldier, but Macaulay himself when in India had gone to great lengths, literally, to get a priest to attend the last moments of a dying Catholic servant. But the passage also turns on death far distant from loved associations, and on the reinforcement of old human loyalties by the nostalgic force of religious observance. He would have liked to think that Margaret's dying moments had been strengthened by happy memories of the religious household of Clapham, pre-eminent among them her deeply loved eldest brother. These little touches in his writing henceforward provide an invaluable additional artistic dimension, but for his biography their main service is to emphasize the deepening of Macaulay's creative processes at their most personal. On the other hand, his *Edinburgh* essays on Robert Clive (January 1840) and Warren Hastings (October 1841) were obvious enough consequences of his Indian experience. The sketch of Lord Holland (July 1841), recently dead, with background silhouettes of his uncle Charles and his grandfather Henry Fox, again had an obvious origin, but its nature told how much of the world Macaulay had known before his departure had now passed away: he could be Mr Macaulay, the youthful sage of Holland House, no longer. His essay on Leigh Hunt's edition of Restoration comedy (January 1841) was again more intimate at its point of greatest vehemence, his conviction of the grossly insulting treatment of women by Congreve, Wycherley and their fellows: the thought of woman as a sex object was a horror to him particularly in his mourning for Margaret. And we have seen how his repressed sense of English Scotophobia was finally released in his last *Edinburgh* essay in 1844 (p. 22 above), again a fruit of the private impulses of creativity.[31]

Another of these last *Edinburgh* essays, that on Ranke's *History of the Popes* (October 1840), was prompted by a more recent personal experience. From October 1838 to January 1839 he travelled through France and Italy, spending some six weeks in the Papal States. He was pressing ahead with his *Lays of Ancient Rome*, using his journey to round out topographical material in 'Horatius' and receiving initial inspiration for 'The Prophecy of Capys', as well as recording impressions which would surface in the other two, 'Virginia' and 'The Battle of Lake Regillus'. His journal, now in active and lengthy compilation, is an excellent and at times very amusing account of his observations: sometimes he found what he had envisaged, sometimes he was confirmed in his opinions, sometimes he was surprised by his discoveries. Although it possesses many private reflections, and evidently included many more on Margaret removed after his death by Hannah, there is an oddly public quality about the writing. It is assertive, as his public discourse in speech or print is assertive. The presence of another, less assured, Macaulay is at times near enough to the surface to be inferred: but writing for him was a means of stating conclusions, not of resolving doubts, still less of leaving them unresolved. His attitude to Roman Catholicism seems a case in point. He made many testy observations about the bad social conditions of the Papal States, about the pernicious effects of clerical power, about the obvious prevalence of superstition, about the poor Latin and bad singing in Catholic services; he was in raptures about St Peter's; and he took a schoolboy satisfaction in having his bow acknowledged by Pope Gregory XVI. But he went to Mass again and again throughout the tour, studied the service with care, and wept at the *Stabat Mater* while mocking himself for a reaction which would surely have moved the mirth of Virgil and Cicero. There is every evidence for his utter contempt for the intellectual basis of Roman Catholic theology in its unique particulars; but he was evidently fascinated by its emotional pull on its votaries, wished to understand it, and apparently experienced a little of it. He admired the preaching of the future Roman Catholic Archbishop of Westminster, Nicholas Wiseman, but found it curiously unEnglish. He made investigations of the Jesuits' indifference to the danger of death in their solicitude for comforting the sick and dying during a terrible plague outbreak in the very recent past: this would have had a slight impact on his use of the example of the dying Irish soldier and more directly informed his discussion of the Jesuits in the Ranke essay and the *History*. The whole episode has almost nothing in common with the mood which led so many English intellectuals of his day to embrace Roman Catholicism – many of the children of his father's fellow Evangelicals among them – save perhaps for his respect for the religious devotion so plain among so many Catholics. But it testifies to his anxiety to understand something of the emotional basis for ideology, more particularly ideology of religious origin: his own experience in the Clapham Sect household of his youth had taught him some of the same lessons in relation to Evangelical Protestantism. Here he seems much more concerned to observe the process than to imagine he can find the answer.[32]

After his return and absorption in Ellis's tragedy, he found himself being called back into public life. He was elected to the Reform Club and – what he valued much more – to The Club, once famous for being the formal meeting-place of Johnson, Burke and their circle. He was invited to stand for Parliament in Edinburgh and was elected on 4 June 1839. He took Ellis to Paris in September, and composed his brief poem on the *Flying Dutchman* theme, 'The Last Buccaneer', to amuse his friend who had been made seasick by the Channel storms which in the same season carried Wagner to the coast of Norway, thus leading him to choose that as his location for the opera he was currently composing on the same tradition: it is a striking reminder of Macaulay's part-share in the climate of European romanticism.

> The winds were yelling, the waves were swelling,
>   The sky was black and drear,
> When the crew with eyes of flame brought the ship without a
>   name
>   Alongside the last Buccaneer ...[33]

He found awaiting him when he returned to London an invitation from Lord Melbourne to join the Cabinet as Secretary-at-War; he accepted and was sworn of the Privy Council on 30 September. He held office for two years. For his future *History* the experience was invaluable, although the Cabinet had changed dramatically even since his early days in Westminster: Melbourne had introduced the principle of the collective responsibility of the Cabinet, which Macaulay would have applauded in principle but may have found a little onerous in practice. He was far from finding his colleagues the happy band of brothers he had served with such oratorical zeal in the great days of Reform. Individual tensions and personal ambitions were rising; collective morale was low. Macaulay's former patron and subsequent enemy Brougham was now outside the Ministry, left to waste thirty more years of a brilliant but factious mind in isolation. The rising figure was Palmerston, whose vigorous foreign policy, in its jealousy for British glory and its support for international liberalism, Macaulay found more congenial than the views of any other minister, but Palmerston himself was suspected of dealing with the Tory Opposition to safeguard his office. For a time only Queen Victoria's preference for Melbourne kept the administration in power. It faced a bitterly hostile Opposition, growing in strength, supported by strong anti-Catholic sentiment in the country all the more strident because of the Cabinet's private understanding with Daniel O'Connell, and noisy enough in the House of Commons to howl Macaulay's speeches into inaudibility, though not silence. He had been a giant of the Reform crisis; and the generation ultimately produced by that crisis did not know him, and did not seem to want to. He persevered, and kept his courage and his head when the press followed the Opposition in their vilifications, an outcry proving particularly vehement when he absentmindedly if accurately employed his temporary address, Windsor Castle, on a public letter announcing his candidacy for re-election, a procedure required in those days on acceptance of government office. He was nevertheless re-elected without difficulty. As Secretary-at-War, he had to defend many of the worst abuses of the unreformed army. He also defended, with more enthusiasm, the Opium War into which the United Kingdom had been drawn against China. Significantly, he did so by use of his moral yardstick, the struggle against slavery:

> Take a parallel case: take the most execrable crime that was ever called a trade, the African slave trade.... suppose, Sir, that a ship under French colours was seen skulking near the [British] island [of Mauritius], that the Governor was fully satisfied from her build, her rigging, and her movements, that she was a slaver, and was only waiting for the night to put on shore the wretches who were in her hold. Suppose that, not having a sufficient naval force to seize this vessel, he were to arrest thirty or forty French

merchants, most of whom had never been suspected of slave-trading, and were to lock them up. Suppose that he were to lay violent hands on the French consul. Suppose that the Governor were to threaten to starve his prisoners to death unless they produced the proprietor of the slaver. Would not the French Government in such a case have a right to demand reparation? And, if we refused reparation, would not the French Government have a right to exact reparation by arms?

He made it clear that this was no matter of protocol:

> Conscious of superior power, we can bear to hear our Sovereign described as a tributary of the Celestial Empire. Conscious of superior knowledge we can bear to hear ourselves described as savages destitute of every useful art. When our ambassadors were required to perform a prostration, which in Europe would have been considered as degrading, we were rather amused than irritated.... But this is not a question of phrases and ceremonies. The liberties and lives of Englishmen are at stake: and it is fit that all nations, civilised and uncivilised, should know that, wherever the Englishman may wander, he is followed by the eye and guarded by the power of England.

The speech (7 April 1840) symbolizes the tension, and perhaps the turning-point, in Macaulay's preachment of reform and nationalism. Had his private and public sentiments been accompanied by calls for a crusade for greater efforts to curtail the odious traffic in opium, it would have done more honour to his inheritance. As it was, British success in the war remained his focus, and when victory was achieved against China, and in the simultaneous wars with Egypt and with Afghanistan, he wrote to his fellow Whig Lord Ebrington on 6 January 1841: 'Glorious news from all corners of the world. If we go out now, we go out with all the honours of war – drums beating and colours flying.' The Parliament was not in fact dissolved until June; Macaulay was re-elected at Edinburgh but the Ministry was forced to resign on 30 August. On the whole he welcomed it: the previous survival on a mere five votes had been a wearing business, and the ironic dependence on Royal favour by the Whig adversaries of George IV and critics of William IV had been degrading. He thought kindly of Victoria, but never imagined her to be remotely near the intellectual level of any of his sisters: when presented to her in 1839 he reported to one of them that he 'had the honour of a conversation with her of about two minutes, and assured her that India was hot'.[34]

He moved to the Albany, Piccadilly, and now began intensive research work on the great project which would dominate the remaining twenty years of his life, the *History of England*. He had sketched his idea of it on 20 July 1838 to Macvey Napier, who had edited the *Edinburgh* since 1829:

> The first part of which, I think, will take up five octavo volumes will extend from the Revolution [of 1688] to the commencement of Sir Robert Walpole's long Administration, – a period of three or four and thirty very eventful years. From the commencement of Walpole's administration to the commencement of the American war, events may be dispatched more concisely. From the commencement of the American war it will again become necessary to be copious. These at least are my present notions. How far I shall bring the narrative down I have not determined. The death of George the Fourth would be the best halting place. The History would then be an entire view of all the transactions which took place between the revolution which brought the Crown into harmony with the parliament and the revolution which brought the parliament into harmony with the nation. But there are great and obvious objections to contemporary history. To be sure, if I live to be seventy, the events of George the Fourth's reign will be to me then what the American war and the Coalition [of Fox and North which followed it] are to me now.

He was to persist in this design as late as 1848, when his first two volumes were published, announcing his proposed length of coverage at their commencement. But these two only brought him to the formal conclusion of the Revolution in England, with the proclamation of William III and Mary II. He had covered in detail the reign of James II which began in 1685. His next two volumes, published in December 1855, brought him to the Peace of Ryswick in 1697. His fifth volume would not appear until after his death; its coverage of the final two years of William III's reign only existed in fragments, and it ended with William's death in 1702. Had Macaulay survived to continue at the same rate of progress, he would have reached Walpole's acceptance of office in 1721 by the time he was seventy, and would have run to more than twice the length he originally assumed. Its further continuation along the lines he proposed would have finished when he was well over a hundred. Although the chronological span actually covered by the *History* was very short, little more than fifteen or sixteen years, we must think of his work in the 1840s as carried out in the expectation of concluding it within living memory, and notice that he made little initial distinction between events before his birth and those in his lifetime. His interviews and conversation with witnesses of the politics and society of the reign of George III must have strengthened that sense of his own presence in the past. So must conversation with his father on Highland tradition. His first research trip, in August 1842, was to Devonshire and Somerset to visit the scenes of Monmouth's Rebellion at the beginning of James II's reign, and here he took oral testimony also as to traditions on the revolt, noting that there had been little movement of population in Somerset in the previous century and a half. So we must envisage him at work during the succeeding years, striving to see and hear the events he was researching and describing. From now on, the story of his life is that of a man whose energies are increasingly given to living in the 1680s and 1690s rather than in his own time.[35]

His own time did not so easily give up its demands on his attention. His *Lays of Ancient Rome* appeared in October 1842, and became a universal favourite. He had prefaced it with a scholarly discussion of the lost folk ballads in which the early Romans sang of the heroic struggles they imagined in order to entertain their leisure and enlarge their pride, and which Livy and Dionysius of Halicarnassus later wove into the openings of their histories; but it was the lays rather than their preface that captured the audience. The fashion of declamation was then at its height, and the child of the family which had read aloud so much was naturally prepared for his work. The poems were engulfed in, and swelled, the tide of Romanticism then roaring across Europe and North America, and what Macaulay had intended partly as a poetic contrivance became pure celebration in the minds of his readers and hearers. His own growing popularity led to American piracies of his work, and their intrusion into Britain obliged him to collect those of the *Edinburgh* essays he deemed to merit a permanent life. Here again the force of his early, unabashed Romanticism in 'Milton' and its more controlled expression in later essays now joined that found in the *Lays* to give further nourishment to the prevailing mood.

But in Parliament he moved into a different role, that of the prematurely elder statesman. This was no mere business of Opposition advocacy, such as that on which he had cut his Parliamentary teeth for a few months in 1830. He was now transformed from a minor minister in a discredited and mortally wounded government into an avenging angel, when it pleased him, dogging the Peel administration with visions of the poor figure it cut in historical perspective. The youngsters who had howled him down were now to see their august chief grow pale under the magisterial roll of Macaulay's oratorical thunder. The historian was the man of the moment, with his *Critical and Historical Essays* in every well-appointed library and his *Lays of Ancient Rome* in every fashionable drawing room. He whose incessant discourse had been the rueful despair of his political and literary colleagues now made his hearers hunger for one of his speeches. The Commons seemed hardly to possess his equal, especially after the aged Daniel O'Connell was removed and broken by imprisonment in 1844 and the former Whig and present Tory Minister Stanley went to the Lords the same year. Macaulay was implacably opposed to O'Connell's crusade for repeal of the Union between Britain and Ireland, but all the more did he therefore insist on the removal of impediments to Irish equality of opportunity in the United Kingdom. Peel's prosecution of O'Connell was motivated in part by his own long antipathy to the Irish leader, in part by his fear of Stanley, whose movement to the Tory right would ultimately lead to their rupture. Macaulay, at work on the *History* which would state in its opening paragraphs that Ireland was the great failure in the 150 years of English progress from 1688, still continued his efforts in the hope of ultimate integration of Celt and Saxon. 'It was no common person that you were bent on punishing,' he told Peel in his Commons speech of 19 February 1844:

> it is impossible for me not to see that the place which he holds in the estimation of his countrymen is such as no popular leader in our history, I might perhaps say in the history of the world, has ever attained.... An insurrection in Ireland would have the good wishes of a great majority of the people of Europe.... the cause of the Irish repealers has two different aspects, a democratic

aspect, and a Roman Catholic aspect, and is therefore regarded with favour by foreigners of almost every shade of opinion.... on an occasion on which all Christendom was watching your conduct with an unfriendly and suspicious eye, you should have carefully avoided everything that looked like foul play. Unhappily you were too much bent on gaining the victory; and you have gained a victory more disgraceful and disastrous than any defeat. Mr O'Connell has been convicted: but you cannot deny that he has been wronged: you cannot deny that irregularities have been committed, or that the effect of those irregularities has been to put you in a better situation and him in a worse situation than the law contemplated.

The Lords overturned O'Connell's conviction on appeal, undoubtedly bearing in mind Macaulay's insistence that British law must be dispensed without blemish if it is to command either the allegiance of all its subjects or the respect of foreign powers. If his thoughts still turned much on British prestige, he tried to affirm its joint dependence on military might and on good conscience with rather more consistency when he had no Opium War on his own hands.[36]

Macaulay made very clear the limits of what he meant by Parliament's being brought into harmony with 'the nation' in 1832, when some ten years later he discussed the demands of the Chartists. He agreed with them about a secret ballot instead of the existing vocal declaration of votes, and about abolition of pecuniary qualifications for MPs. But, he said tersely in his speech of 3 May 1842, 'The essence of the Charter is universal suffrage. If you withhold that, it matters not very much what else you grant. If you grant that, it matters not at all what else you withhold. If you grant that, the country is lost.' His argument was that without education persons without property would see no reason for respecting it, and the result would be the destruction of national prosperity.

Our honest working man has not received such an education as enables him to understand that the utmost distress that he has ever known is prosperity when compared with the distress which he would have to endure if there were a single month of general anarchy and plunder. But you say, it is not the fault of the labourer that he is not well educated. Most true. It is not his fault. But though he has no share in the fault, he will, if you are foolish enough to give him supreme power in the state, have a very large share of the punishment.... What we are asked to do is to give universal suffrage before there is universal education. Have I any unkind feeling towards these poor people? No more than I have to a sick friend who implores me to give him a glass of water which the physician has forbidden. No more than a humane collector in India has to these poor peasants who in a season of scarcity crowd round the granaries and beg with tears and piteous gestures that the doors may be opened and the rice distributed. I would not give the draught of water, because I know it would be poison. I would not give up the keys of the granary, because I know that, by doing so, I should turn a scarcity into a famine. And in the same way I would not yield to the importunity of multitudes who, exasperated by suffering and blinded by ignorance, demand with wild vehemence the liberty to destroy themselves.

He had occasionally, with memories of his own Evangelical upbringing in mind, contemplated an England returned to primitive savagery as an event which might well happen before institutions as long-surviving as Greek culture or the Papacy showed any diminution in their hold on human minds and hearts. The rule of the ignorant offered him its occasion:

There would be many millions of human beings, crowded in a narrow space, deprived of all those resources which alone had made it possible for them to exist in so narrow a space; trade gone; manufactures gone; credit gone. What could they do but fight for the mere sustenance of nature, and tear each other to pieces till famine, and pestilence following in the train of famine, came to turn the terrible commotion into a more terrible repose? The best event, the very best event, that I can anticipate, – and what must the state of things be, if an Englishman and a Whig calls such an event the very best? – the very best event, I say, that I can anticipate is that out of the confusion a strong military despotism may arise, and that the sword, firmly grasped by some rough hand, may give a sort of protection to the miserable wreck of all that immense prosperity and glory.

The passage is one that has an eerie foretaste of Yeats's 'The Second

Coming', so much so that – for all of Yeats's rudeness about Whig-gery – it must be presumed a point of origin:

> But, as to the noble institutions under which our country has made such progress in liberty, in wealth, in knowledge, in arts, do not deceive yourselves into the belief that we should ever see them again. We should never see them again. We should not deserve to see them. All those nations which envy our greatness would insult our downfall, a downfall which would be all our own work; and the history of our calamities would be told thus: Eng-land had institutions which, though imperfect, yet contained within themselves the means of remedying every imperfection; those institutions her legislators wantonly and madly threw away....[37]

Macaulay had hitherto been the vociferous enemy of governmen-tal intervention in society, but on education he became more and more conspicuous in demanding governmental assistance. He sup-ported Peel in seeking to establish non-denominational university education in Ireland; he opposed his requirement of theological tests for the universities of Scotland; he supported him in increasing the grant to St Patrick's College, Maynooth, for the education of Irish priests. This last support he coupled on 14 April 1845 with choice language against the Tories who in Opposition had become reinvigorated on anti-Catholic mob support, and now had been forced to increase a grant whose existence they had opposed:

> The natural consequences follow. All those fierce spirits, whom you hallooed on to harass us, now turn round and begin to worry you. The Orangeman raises his war-whoop: Exeter Hall sets up its bray: Mr Macneile shudders to see more costly cheer than ever provided for the priests of Baal at the table of the Queen; and the Protestant Operatives of Dublin call for impeachments in exceedingly bad English. But what did you expect? Did you think, when, to serve your turn, you called the Devil up, that it was as easy to lay him as to raise him? Did you think, when you went on, session after session, thwarting and reviling those whom you knew to be in the right, and flattering all the worst passions of those whom you knew to be in the wrong, that the day of reckoning would never come? It has come. There you sit, doing penance for the disingenuousness of years....

But, however unwelcome the candour of such an ally might be to Peel, he could be relied on. His peroration was evidently conceived with the recollection of Burke's speech in the Bristol Guildhall on the eve of the 1780 election, when he was defeated because of his support for earlier measures of Catholic relief:

I know well that the fate of this bill and the fate of the administration are in our hands. But far be it from us to imitate the arts by which we were overthrown.... If this bill, having been introduced by Tories, shall be rejected by Whigs, both the great parties in the State will be alike discredited. There will be one vast shipwreck of all the public character in the country. Therefore, making up my mind to sacrifices, which are not unattended with pain, and repressing some feelings which stir strongly within me, I have determined to give my strenuous support to this bill. Yes, Sir, to this bill, and to every bill which shall seem to be likely to promote the real Union of Great Britain and Ireland, I will give my support, regardless of obloquy, regardless of the risk which I may run of losing my seat in Parliament. For such obloquy I have learned to consider as true glory; and as to my seat I am determined that it shall never be held by an ignominious tenure; and I am sure that it can never be lost in a more honourable cause.

He proved a true prophet. He was indeed successful at Edinburgh on 14 July 1846, when he went forward for the then statutory re-election on being made Paymaster-General of the Forces in the administration formed by Lord John Russell after the fall of Peel, but when Parliament was dissolved in 1847 his opponents were prepared for him. It was not his vote for the increased Maynooth grant which proved decisive – a Whig running-mate was re-elected despite a silent vote for it – but his speeches, his luxurious language in dissection of bigotry, and his ability to state his case in forms more appositely Biblical than his opponents'. Several interest-groups had mutually conflicting reasons to be angry with him, but he owed his ouster above all to the anti-Catholic opponents whom he had collectively termed 'the Devil', and who owed it to themselves to show their unconquerable will and study of revenge. He was defeated on 30 July 1847 and sent his public letter to the electors on 2 August:

Gentlemen,

You have been pleased to dismiss me from your service, and I submit to your pleasure without repining. The generous kindness of those who to the last gave me their support I shall always remember with gratitude. If anything has occurred of which I might justly complain, I have forgiven and shall soon forget it.

The points on which we have differed I leave with confidence to the judgment of my country. I cannot expect that you will at present admit my views to be correct; but the time will come when you will calmly review the history of my connection with Edinburgh. You will then, I am convinced, acknowledge that if I incurred your displeasure, I incurred it by remaining faithful to the general interests of the Empire, and to the fundamental principles of the Constitution. I shall always be proud to think that I once enjoyed your favour. But permit me to say, I shall remember not less proudly how I risked and how I lost it.

With every wish for the peace and prosperity of your City,

I have the honour to be,

Gentlemen,

Your faithful servant,

T.B.Macaulay.[38]

He absolutely refused alternative offers of Parliamentary seats. He continued to discharge his ministerial duties, which were small, until 25 April 1848, when he quietly resigned. His fine spirit in public, and his brave letters to Hannah and Ellis, disguised the depth of the wound. As an additional knife-twist the candidate who had displaced him was then disqualified on a technicality but was re-elected without opposition, Macaulay having from the first told supporters and relatives that 'no consideration shall induce me to be again a candidate for Edinburgh'. A private poem he wrote soon afterwards envisions his being addressed as an infant by the spirit who gave him 'The sense of beauty and the love of truth ...' when the Queens of Gain, Fashion, Power and Pleasure passed him by. (The sneer of Fashion, 'More scornful still' than Gain, is a nice indication that Macaulay's sense of humour had not deserted him: Beau Brummel ran no risk of competition from him.) Although his letter to the Edinburgh electors had put his cause in terms of imperial interest and the fundamental principles of the Constitution – firmly placing equality of opportunity for Irish Catholics by provision of education for their clergy within that context, in clear defiance of the zealots who asserted the Constitution's unalterable Protestantism since the Revolution of 1688 – his 'Lines Written in August' was much more explicit about what he took to be the circumstances of his defeat, as the spirit promises him she will be:

> Thine most, when friends turn pale, when traitors fly,
>   When, hard beset, thy spirit, justly proud,
> For truth, peace, freedom, mercy, dares defy
>   A sullen priesthood and a raving crowd.
>
> Amidst the din of all things fell and vile,
>   Hate's yell, and envy's hiss, and folly's bray,
> Remember me; and with an unforced smile
>   See riches, baubles, flatterers, pass away.
>
> Yes: they will pass away; nor deem it strange;
>   They come and go, as comes and goes the sea:
> And let them come and go; thou, through all change,
>   Fix thy firm gaze on virtue and on me.

Thus it ended, leaving unstated who the spirit actually is. But one verse told of the dominion with which he accredited her, and what he sought from her:

> Without one envious sigh, one anxious scheme,
>   The nether sphere, the fleeting hour resign.
> Mine is the world of thought, the world of dream,
>   Mine all the past, and all the future mine.

The particular significance of this relates to the *History*: Macaulay wanted to write something that would be read in a thousand years' time. His own favourite historian, Thucydides, had written his work over 2,250 years earlier. In his intentions, Macaulay is the pre-eminent time-traveller.[39]

Defeat intensified Macaulay's return to the past. He set off for the Netherlands with the faithful Ellis to ransack the Dutch archives, at that date possibly the most professionally administered national archives in the world. He had been at work in the State Paper Office in London since January 1842. His old friend Sir James Mackintosh had planned a history of the Revolution of 1688, leaving a fragment to be published after his death (reviewed by Macaulay for the *Edinburgh* where his essay appeared in July 1835), and had assembled a vast body of document transcriptions from widely scattered sources, including the archives of France, Spain, the Netherlands and the letters of the Papal nuncio during James II's years; the collection also included manuscript newsletters sent from London to be perused by selected groups of squirearchical and clerical readers in the provinces. These had been put in Macaulay's custody by Mackintosh's heirs before he announced his projected *History* to Napier in July 1838. The Hollands made available to him Charles James Fox's published and unpublished transcripts of French diplomatic despatches from the envoys of Louis XIV at the Courts of Charles II and James II, and the French, as well as the Dutch, archives enabled him to fill what he called 'chasms' in the mass of reproduced documents in his possession. Certain sets of despatches and papers had been published, among them invaluable letters sent to the Court of the exiled James in St Germains, after his final exile; these had appeared in Sir John Dalrymple's *Memoirs of Great Britain and Ireland* in the 1770s only to have their originals destroyed in the French Revolution. Apart from his researches in domestic and foreign archives and libraries, then, Macaulay was in an extraordinary situation for primary research at his own fireside. This did not restrain his energetic pursuit of other manuscript and printed sources, such as pamphlets, broadsheets, plays, diaries, digests of newsletters, satires, ballads, lampoons and – once they began to appear – newspapers. Behind the triumphs and ultimate disaster of his intermittent political activity of the 1840s we have to see a constant activity of research. His magnificent memory was laid under terrific strain in the process, and it is clear that he relied on it to excess. He began drafting material in March 1839 and resumed it much more purposefully in November 1841, although he would write five more *Edinburgh* essays within the next three years. By 1848 he was rising at daybreak and sometimes working at the *History* for stretches of twelve hours at a time. The final version was evidently written at breakneck speed in that year, but we have to assume many earlier drafts and differing schemes of procedure over the preceding seven years. Longmans, with whom he signed a contract for £200 a year for five years for 6,000 copies, published the first two volumes on 2 December 1848. It was a runaway success from the moment it went on sale; we shall examine possible reasons later.[40]

Macaulay had accepted a candidacy for the post of Lord Rector of the University of Glasgow: the candidate did not have to campaign, and the franchise was limited to the students. The contest was normally between figures identified with the major political parties, and his opponent, the incumbent, was a local Tory MP. The contest was taken very seriously by young and old, being a foretaste of the alignment of the politics of the future. The Tories seem to have run a very dirty campaign, involving what Macaulay afterwards termed a 'silly calumny', possibly an imputation that he was about to turn Roman Catholic and probably to do with his political martyrdom on the Maynooth grant. Macaulay had a majority of 255 over 203, and carried all four 'nations', as the divisions of the electoral college were called. He delivered his rectorial address after his installation on 21 March 1849, paid a graceful compliment to his opponent, and made his theme the University of Glasgow itself, as its quatercentenary was at hand. If the Glasgow students had intended to show their superiority to the bigotry of the Edinburgh electorate, they were to see that defeat had led their man to strike none of his colours. Glasgow, like all pre-Reformation universities, had been founded on a Papal Bull, and fortunately the Pope in question had been

a man, never to be mentioned without reverence by every lover of letters.... Our just attachment to that Protestant faith to which our country owes so much must not prevent us from paying the tribute which, on this occasion, and in this place, justice and gratitude demand, to the founder of the University of Glasgow, the greatest of the restorers of learning, Pope Nicholas the Fifth. He had sprung from the common people; but his abilities and his erudition, had early attracted the notice of the great. He had studied much and travelled far. He had visited Britain, which, in wealth and refinement, was to his native Tuscany what the back settlements of America now are to Britain. He had lived with the merchant princes of Florence, those men who first ennobled trade by making trade the ally of philosophy, of eloquence, and of taste. It was he who, under the protection of the munificent

47

and discerning Cosmo, arranged the first public library that Modern Europe possessed.... By him was founded the Vatican library, then and long after the most precious and the most extensive collection of books in the world. By him were carefully preserved the most valuable intellectual treasures which had been snatched from the wreck of the Byzantine empire.... By him were introduced to the knowledge of Western Europe two great and unrivalled models of historical composition, the work of Herodotus and the work of Thucydides....[41]

It is worth dwelling for a moment on the personal loyalties which the passage brings together. Firstly, Macaulay was now a scholar, himself without offspring, but living in the hope of educating and entertaining posterity, of which the students were, so to say, an advance guard. His method was, as always, that of fascinating his audience by a wealth of exciting reference, lucid in its outlines, while inviting his hearers to future researches on his more arcane allusions. It linked pride of place and grand associations of local institutional history to international literature, scholarship and history. It paid tribute to the spirit of commerce, but insisted on its self-justification by furtherance of culture. It singled out the ideal of the poor boy of talent rising to his due reward by his studies and ideals, a point in which his own convictions and the Scottish tradition of education for the 'lad o' pairts' were happily in conjunction (thanks to Zachary). It saluted the ideal of the public civic library, and of the great archival library. It brooded tenderly over the custody of cultural artefacts endangered by war, by ignorance and by lack of communications. It saluted his beloved great historians of Greece and Rome. And it quietly evangelized its audience in its various causes, in the context of an argument that the love of learning must not only show itself the foe of religious or ethnic bigotry but must positively revere those who had advanced human knowledge from any civilization, however alien to the hearers.

He proceeded from here to his great gospel of improvement and progress, and it may have been that the grasp he showed of Scottish history and literature, firm if slight, had a hidden sense of possession in that this was the institution which served the West of Scotland whence his own ancestors had come. (In the Hebrides its hinterland had a rival in that of the University of Aberdeen.) Glasgow offered him a theme, in the advancement of industrial prosperity and of the Scottish Enlightenment. It was a conjunction in which he deeply believed, and here uniquely could it be found. He had rejoiced in the newly found prosperity and significance of his former Parliamentary seat in Leeds; but it was as yet no centre of learning. He had rejoiced in the cultural strength of his former Parliamentary seat in Edinburgh with its Enlightenment, its *Encyclopaedia Britannica*, its University, its medical school, its legal nursery, its *Review* and – when not tied to a wounding narrowness of theological sectarianism – its learning; but it was no product of industrial revolution. Glasgow, whose past he now surveyed through brief glimpses at the span of each century, spoke to both parts of his deeply urban nature. And he therefore gave to Glasgow one of his happiest appeals to the future when he spoke of the prospects that might lie before his successor in 1949. He scouted alarmists:

Ever since I began to make observations on the state of my country I have been seeing nothing but growth, and hearing of nothing but decay. The more I contemplate our noble institutions, the more convinced I am that they are sound at heart, that they have nothing of age but its dignity, and that their strength is still the strength of youth. The hurricane [the 1848 revolutions], which has recently overthrown so much that was great and that seemed durable, has only proved their solidity. They still stand, august and immovable, while dynasties and churches are lying in heaps of ruin all around us. I see no reason to doubt that, by the blessing of God on a wise and temperate policy, on a policy of which the principle is to preserve what is good by reforming in time what is evil, our civil institutions may be preserved uninjured to a late posterity, and that, under the shade of our civil institutions, our academical institutions may long continue to flourish.

... My successor will, I hope, be able to boast that the fifth century of the University has even been more glorious than the fourth. He will be able to vindicate that boast by citing a long list of eminent men, great masters of experimental science, of ancient learning, of our native eloquence, ornaments of the senate, the pulpit and the bar. He will, I hope, mention with high honour some of my young friends who now hear me; and he will, I also hope, be able to add that their talents and learning were not wasted on selfish or ignoble objects, but were employed to promote the physical and moral good of their species, to extend the empire of man over the material world, to defend the cause of civil and religious liberty against tyrants and bigots, and to defend the cause of virtue and order against the enemies of all divine and human laws.

These were the values which Macaulay sought to teach the Victorians, and we would do well to remember his idea of the purpose of a university.[42]

Macaulay was pleased by the reception of his speech, telling Lady Theresa Lewis on 28 March, 'It produced an effect as great as the lyre of Orpheus. For it prevented the boys from pelting the Professors with peas, an effect never before, within living memory, achieved by any orator.' He was breaking other records too: his *History* had by now sold 13,000 copies in Britain, and American sales were reaching 100,000. He travelled from Glasgow to Edinburgh for what would be his last meeting with his first *Edinburgh* editor, Francis (now Lord) Jeffrey, to whom he had dedicated his *Critical and Historical Essays* and whose critical opinion he had sought for the *History* when it was in proof stage. In July he refused the Regius Professorship of Modern History at Cambridge. In August he travelled to Ireland to examine the major locations of his future narrative of the revolutionary conflicts of 1688–91 in that country, and if the local traditions were of less use to him than in Somerset he found an invaluable ally in the great topographer of the Boyne Dr William Wilde, future father of Oscar Wilde. He gallantly, if somewhat bemusedly, joined Wilde in subsequent after-dinner singing, and shrewdly noted that Dublin society preserved such Regency fashions which had fallen into disfavour in London. (The remark explains a good deal about mid-century Anglo-Irish life, not least as manifested in the Wilde family.) He set out in September with Ellis to study in the French archives. His health began to decline, but in summer 1850 he was back in Scotland to investigate the major sites of his narrative. His scientific attempts in these journeys did him credit, but the artistic intent was even more important. To get himself into the heart of the events he described, he wanted to inform his imagination. His tour would end in the footsteps of his grandfather, at Inverary. But Scotland had another call on him. He allowed his name to go forward for re-election for Edinburgh on the strict understanding that he would make no campaign whatsoever, would make no pledges, and would return any enquiries as to his future voting conduct with a polite refusal to answer. Apart from the principle involved he was in any case wise: his victory at the head of the poll on 13 July 1852 was followed by another heart attack. He was unable even to travel to Edinburgh to meet his constituents until November, and took his seat in the same month. But he kept on with his *History* and began writing his fourth volume in January 1853.[43]

The Commons, where he spoke but seldom, took up little of his time: both Edinburgh and he well knew that his vindication had been an act of civic honour and atonement rather than any serious call to further service. But the *History* was interrupted for two other projects. One, the publication of his *Speeches*, was occasioned by a circumstance that annoyed him intensely: a badly mangled edition of his speeches was issued by Henry Vizetelly, claiming to have been produced under special licence. In his preface to his own edition Macaulay declared of the Vizetelly volume:

> The substance of what I said is perpetually misrepresented. The connection of the arguments is altogether lost. Extravagant blunders are put into my mouth in almost every page....
>
> I cannot permit myself to be exhibited, in this ridiculous and degrading manner, for the profit of an unprincipled man....
>
> I have only, in conclusion, to beg that the readers of this Preface will pardon an egotism which a great wrong has made necessary, and which is quite as disagreeable to myself as it can be to them.

He reminded his readers that he was a very difficult man to report, given his rapid delivery, and that while seeking to avoid any revision of the sentiments he believed he had expressed regardless of any subsequent modification, he could vouch for the accuracy of only nine Parliamentary texts, corrected by him within a week of their delivery. 'Many expressions, and a few paragraphs, linger in my memory. But the rest, including much that had been carefully pre-meditated, is irrecoverably lost.... As I am unable to recall the precise words which I used, I have done my best to put my meaning into words which I might have used.' His *History* had contained no preface, but this was the principle on which conversations obviously not based on verbatim reporting were included in its pages. Macaulay was something of an impressionist in default of fuller evidence; on the other hand, he did not follow his hero Thucydides in attributing orations to anyone other than himself. The *Speeches* appeared in December 1853. Unlike his *Critical and Historical Essays*, there would be no new material to be added to later editions.

Macaulay derived much more pleasure from the other interruption in the work 'which is the business and pleasure of my life'. One of his most famous and faithful votaries in Edinburgh, the publisher Adam Black, twice Lord Provost and Macaulay's successor in 1856 as MP, persuaded him to write some biographies for the *Encyclopaedia Britannica*. Macaulay supplied five in all, *Francis Atterbury, John Bunyan, Oliver Goldsmith, Samuel Johnson* and *William Pitt. Bunyan* and *Johnson* went over ground already opened by him in the *Edinburgh* in 1831, on the two great voices from the English lower classes, and throw much light on the maturing of his style, his temper and his critical perception. *Atterbury* is a hostile sketch of a Jacobite Anglican bishop of the early eighteenth century. *Goldsmith* is an agreeable and constructively critical narrative, notable for its haunting and well-informed allusion to early Gaelic influence at the commencement, and for its fine appreciation of 'Retaliation' at the close. But the essay on the hero of his boyhood from whom he had been so long alienated, the younger Pitt, is a masterly biography. Concluded in August 1858, it also has the melancholy interest of being his last completed work. And it reflects the influence of a literary friendship maintained for over twenty years with Pitt's grand-nephew Philip Henry, Lord Mahon, later Earl Stanhope. Mahon was Macaulay's only close Tory friend; ironically, Macaulay's review of his *History of the War of the Succession in Spain* (*Edinburgh*, January 1833) is much less partial to the Whig side in disputes of Queen Anne's reign than is Mahon, conscious of his descent from Whig leaders of that day. Stanhope's massive *Life of Pitt*, which appeared after Macaulay's death, speaks with an eloquent affection for the Macaulay biography of its subject; thereby it constitutes an exception to the writings by descendants of persons whose history had come under Macaulay's scrutiny: in place of the usual remonstrances against the wide circulation of his critical judgments, there is an eloquent affection for Macaulay's essay.

The third and fourth volumes of the *History* were published on 17 December 1855, in a first edition of 25,000 copies. Macaulay retired from the House of Commons at the end of January 1856.

Longmans paid £20,000 into his account in March. In May he began a full correction of the *History* for the seven-volume edition to be published in 1857–58. He also left his Albany residence for Holly Lodge, Campden Hill, where he began the last and unfinished volume of his *History* in October. He accepted a peerage from Palmerston in 1857 and in December of that year entered the House of Lords as Baron Macaulay of Rothley. He continued to travel on the Continent with Ellis each year until 1859 when, learning to his great grief that Hannah was to travel to India to be with her husband in his new appointment there, he accompanied her on a last visit to Glasgow, Inverary and Edinburgh in the summer. He grew increasingly depressed at her imminent departure, had a further heart attack in December and died on the 28th of that month. Ellis saw an edition of many of his friend's uncollected writings through the press and died fifteen months after him. Hannah brought out the fifth volume of the *History* later in 1861.[44]

2 The Lays of Ancient Rome

Ye good men of the Commons, with loving hearts and
    true
Who stand by the bold Tribunes that still have stood
    by you,
Come, make a circle round me, and mark my tale with
    care,
A tale of what Rome once hath borne, of what Rome
    yet may bear.
This is no Grecian fable of fountains running wine,
Of maids with snaky tresses, or sailors turned to swine.
Here in this very Forum, under the noonday sun,
In sight of all the people, the bloody deed was done.
Old men still creep among us who saw that fearful day,
Just seventy years and seven ago, when the wicked Ten
    bare sway.

> Macaulay, 'Virginia. Fragments of a
> Lay sung in the Forum on the Day
> whereon Lucius Sextius Lateranus
> and Caius Licinius Calvus Stolo were
> Elected Tribunes of the Commons
> the Fifth Time...'

The Lays of Ancient Rome, Macaulay's first published book other than piracies (university publication of the prize poems 'Pompeii' and 'Evening' excepted), is a work of history, and a work of literature. Its method, its preoccupations, its ethics, its paradoxes, its scholarship, its romanticism and its audience are all of importance in their influence and in their insights on his *History*. It is also of major importance in its own right. Twenty-three thousand copies were sold in its first dozen years in the United Kingdom alone, and it held an enthusiastic audience until the Second World War. Some of its lines are apparently immortal, and the idea of Macaulay as time-traveller is rather coarsely reinforced by their use in at least one comic strip ('Buck Rogers') where they were represented as being quoted (inaccurately) in the twenty-fifth century. It won enthusiastic admirers who otherwise hated Macaulay and all they took him to stand for, such as the Young Ireland polemicist John Mitchel; it proved a great inspiration to imitators and parodists led by William Edmonstoune Aytoun, whose political creed was neo-Jacobite and who later helped orchestrate the most enduring attempt at demolition of the *History* (that by John Paget); it entranced bitter enemies, including the Tory Professor John Wilson of Edinburgh, who wrote as the ferocious 'Christopher North', who reviewed it ecstatically, and who left his sick-bed in 1852 to vote for the author. Although its sale was outstripped from the first by Macaulay's much more expensive *History*, the text of the poems, particularly that of 'Horatius', was probably known ultimately to a larger number of hearers and readers than the text of the *History*.

The *Lays* did not conquer everyone. They induced an attack by Matthew Arnold in 1861, in his 'On Translating Homer', which set on foot the highbrow dismissal of Macaulay as a Philistine, a dismissal to be continued with great influence by Arnold's disciple Leslie Stephen, who enshrined it in the *Dictionary of National Biography*. Many, if not most, historians and literary critics were intimidated by Arnold, Stephen and their followers when it came to Macaulay. There was an element of snobbery in it: Lord Grey, one feels, would have agreed with them that Macaulay's place was below the salt, however little chance he had of grasping their reasoning. The Philistine seems, rather inaccurately, to be the *parvenu*. Does not Macaulay, with his ideas of history and poetry for Everyman, black, brown or white, make a mess of an intellectuals' dinnertable? There was an element of generational retaliation on seniors who had carved their way into social prominence: it was almost as though the heirs raised their eyebrows at the pushiness of their forbears, wondering at those who had so easily admitted them. Stephen's grandfather had been Zachary Macaulay's bosom fellow fighter and fellow Scot in the cause of Evangelicalism and anti-slavery. Arnold's father, the famous headmaster of Rugby, was Ellis's exact contemporary, and Macaulay insisted that it was his eulogy for the lays, two of which were read to him in draft by Fanny Macaulay when he was dying, which determined their author on publication. It is no more sensible to hint at an Oedipus complex in Matthew Arnold than in Macaulay (many people do not have Oedipus complexes: Oedipus didn't, for instance), but there seems to be a tinge of jealousy in Arnold at praise given to the *Lays* by his father which his own mature work never received from him, Thomas having died when Matthew was twenty. Matthew Arnold met Macaulay in 1849 in unpromising circumstances: Macaulay was visiting his old political patron, Lord Lansdowne, whose private secretary Arnold had been since 1847. Macaulay, twenty years after his own dependence on Lansdowne's patronage, may have been too ready to lay down the law before the younger man, who now lacked the freedom to reply forcefully to his master's triumphant former *protégé*. And Macaulay, in what he would have meant as kindness, would certainly have told Matthew that Dr Thomas Arnold had with his dying voice pronounced so favourably on 'Horatius' and 'The Prophecy of Capys' that Macaulay was thus induced to publish *The Lays of Ancient Rome*. Matthew was therefore now doubly restrained from expressing any adverse opinion, but twelve years later, with Macaulay scarcely cold in his grave, he would condemn the *Lays* as 'pinchbeck', subsequently singling out with contempt a famous verse of 'Horatius' (which he quoted with no more accuracy than Buck Rogers):

> Then out spake brave Horatius,
>   The captain of the gate:
> 'To all the men upon this earth
>   Death cometh soon or late'

(and here, since I have been reproached with undervaluing Lord Macaulay's *Lays of Ancient Rome*, let me frankly say that, to my mind, a man's power to detect the ring of false metal in these Lays is a good measure of his fitness to give an opinion about poetical matters at all), – I say, Lord Macaulay's

> To all the men upon this earth
>   Death cometh soon or late,

it is hard to read without a cry of pain.

It should be 'To every man upon this earth', and Arnold's failure to detect the ring of his own false metal is a good measure of his fitness to give an opinion about the *Lays* at all. (In fairness to Buck Rogers, *he* made no such claim.) As for the cry of pain, we may concede it to Matthew Arnold, but for different reasons: death was coming soon, horribly soon, to the father who loved the lines, and the thought of that conjunction must always be painful to the son. But it takes him out of the judgment-seat on any reasonable standard of impartial criticism.[45]

Leslie Stephen, unlike the author of 'Dover Beach', had no obvious credentials as a judge of poetry, but this seems to have done little to diminish his influence. He brought in Macaulay as a hearty: 'he knows, too, how to stir the blood of the average Englishman,' wrote Stephen in the *Cornhill* (reprinted in his *Hours in a Library*), possibly remembering the giant who cried 'Fee-fie-fo-fum'.

> He understands most thoroughly the value of concentration, unity, and simplicity. Every speech or essay forms an artistic whole, in which some distinct moral is vigorously driven home by a succession of downright blows. This strong rhetorical instinct is shown conspicuously in the 'Lays of Ancient Rome', which, whatever we might say of them as poetry, are an admirable specimen of rhymed rhetoric.

But in more general terms Macaulay, it seemed, was no poet.

> ... Macaulay's imagination is as definitely limited as his specula-tion. The genuine poet is also a philosopher. He sees intuitively what the recorder evolves by argument...
>
> ... [Macaulay] is insensible to the visions which reveal them-selves only to minds haunted by thoughts of eternity, and delight-ing to dwell in the borderland where dreams blend with realities....
>
> Macaulay, therefore, can be no more a poet in the sense in which the word is applied to Spenser, or to Wordsworth, both of whom he holds to be intolerable bores, than he can be a meta-physician or a scientific thinker.... In common phraseology, he is a Philistine.... There is much that is good in your Philistine....

Despite the charity of this last bracing reassurance, one may see how the sentiments effectively damned Macaulay in the eyes of the academic high tables, the Bloomsbury Group, the Leavis Scrutineers, the critical elites of right and left. It also left his reputation vulnerable as a great historian: was one to quote the historical findings of a rhymester in rhetoric, or cite epigrams on the past by a versifier deficient in poetry? Goliath has left no Psalms, however useful his military prowess.[46]

Stephen connected Macaulay's supposed deficiencies in relation to poetry with those in relation to history. It may be useful to accept the connection, whatever the deficiencies. In passing, Stephen was as much at fault in his assertion of Macaulay's opinion of Spenser as he was in that (quoted above, p. 16) on Wordsworth. Both statements were in sources he should have known; the latter came from Macaulay's essay on Byron, the former in a letter to Leigh Hunt published (1862) in Hunt's *Correspondence*: 'To deny [Spenser] the rank of a great poet would be to shew utter ignorance of all that belongs to the art. But his excellence is not the sort of excellence in which I take especial delight.' Stephen was severely critical of Macaulay's presumed carelessness and bias leading to adverse judgment; he would have done better to pluck out the beam in his own eye (Matthew, 7: 3). Or perhaps he would have done worse: unlike Macaulay's judgments those by Stephen would be widely adopted with little question, especially by the vast number of ignorant writers who would swallow facts and opinions wholesale from the *Dictionary of National Biography*. Stephen, as general editor and author of so many biographical notices, probably dominated the casual allusions of scholars more fully than any writer in the history of the world.[47]

Stephen's accusation that Macaulay was insensible to visions had the justification that Macaulay was assertive in his speeches and in his writings. Yet Macaulay was a haunted man, not solely by his loss of Margaret. In general he kept quiet about his inheritance of Highland folklore, but there are passages in the second lay (the last of the four to be composed), 'The Battle of the Lake Regillus', which should have given Stephen pause. The visions of Castor and Pollux who appear amid the fighting to support the Romans and afterwards bring the news back to Rome and vanish, are one demonstration of Macaulay's powers in conveying human response to the supernatural. This lay's first presentation of Sextus Tarquinius, whose rape of Lucretia ensured the expulsion of the King his father and the creation of the Roman Republic, is another:

Their leader was false Sextus,
   That wrought the deed of shame:
With restless pace and haggard face
   To his last field he came.
Men said he saw strange visions
   Which none beside might see,
And that strange sounds were in his ears
   Which none might hear but he.
A woman fair and stately,
   But pale as are the dead,
Oft through the watches of the night
   Sat spinning by his bed.
And as she plied the distaff,
   In a sweet voice and low,
She sang of great old houses,
   And fights fought long ago.
So spun she, and so sang she,
   Until the east was grey,
Then pointed to her bleeding breast,
   And shrieked, and fled away.

Lafcadio Hearn, a profound commentator on the supernatural in literature, would remark:

> It is because Macaulay had this power, though using it so sparingly, that his work is so great. If he had not been able to write these lines of poetry ... he could not even have made his history of England the living history that it is. A man who has no ghostly feeling can not make anything alive, not even a page of history or a page of oratory.

And the lines, for one reader at least, have the power to bring water to the eyes and a prickling of hair on the scalp which A.E.Housman defined as the signs that one is thinking about poetry.[48]

The Lays of Ancient Rome offers four stories from Roman tradition as recorded by Livy and Dionysius of Halicarnassus, and tells them as they might have been sung by unknown popular bards or reciters: the successful defence of Rome against the invasion to restore the ousted Tarquins led by Lars Porsena of Clusium, the Etruscan King, whose army is stopped by three Romans standing before the bridge over the Tiber while their fellow citizens cut it down from behind ('Horatius'), the defeat of a Latin army attacking Rome in the same cause ('The Battle of the Lake Regillus'); the attempt by a patrician magistrate to seize for carnal purposes the young daughter of a plebeian soldier and her murder by her father when the law is twisted against them ('Virginia'); the prophetic account of the successful warlike career of Rome uttered by a blind seer to its future founder Romulus fresh from killing the great-uncle who had thrown him and his brother Remus as babies into the Tiber, whence they were rescued and suckled by a wolf ('The Prophecy of Capys'). The compositions themselves became so popular that admirers and critics alike continually recalled them without reference to the context in which Macaulay had placed them in his preface. But without it no criticism makes sense of them.

Undoubtedly Macaulay enjoyed writing them, and his conviction that they must be successful in their own right is indicated by his decision to publish in the light of Dr Arnold's enthusiasm for what Fanny read of them. But his enterprise was founded on an extraordinarily bold attempt of imagination. He insisted that the stories themselves were patently fictitious. The Capys prophecy was his own invention, but the story of Romulus, Remus and the wolf which provided its antecedent was an obvious fabrication, quite apart from its insistence that the war-god Mars was the boys' father. Lars Porsena certainly seems to have invaded Rome; unfortunately he also seems to have captured it: the story of the Tarquins and the fate of Lucretia had no known basis in fact. The Romans certainly fought against the Latins on other matters, but presumably without divine assistance. All these supposed events lay long before any historical record, apart from the unpleasing information on Porsena's success to which Roman historians made no allusion. Macaulay was on less certain ground in dismissing the tale of Virginia as fictitious: but he had strong personal reasons for writing it, he saw it as ammunition in the struggle of plebeian against patrician, and it had many of the hallmarks of invention although there may have been good warrant for the tradition that the patrician Appius Claudius had been driven from a powerful magistracy in disgraceful circumstances. Macaulay's purpose was not to give an appearance of fact to what he believed to be invention, but to work out the circumstances in which such legends circulated. He pointed out that songs about such things certainly had existed, and had perished without being written down. Following other authorities he argued that the obviously imaginary origins of Rome as described by its historians must have arisen from these lost songs: it was his task to work his way back to them, partly in deduction, partly in intuition.

His enterprise was to present the ideas, beliefs, attitudes and sense of identity of a people whose forms of community expression were lost, and to do so in a way which would become as accessible as possible to his own contemporaries. The germ of the idea may be traced back in a letter to his mother written the day after his fourteenth birthday. It was prompted by his reading of David Hume's *History of England*, warmly supporting his parents' religious views but building on them. His remarks offer a crucial key to his lifelong sense of his difference from Hume as a historian. Hume's was

> a History equal to any of the Classical Models in elegance, and, except as far as regards religion, superior to them in authenticity... disgraced by the utter want of religious principle. This is a disadvantage, I think, not only as it tends to misrepresent those subjects in comparison of which history is unimportant, but as it takes away from the interest of the work. Livy and Herodotus believe all the stories of their Jupiters and Minervas; – so that in reading their histories we see that they enter into the spirit of the time, and yet can separate between what is true and what is false. Hume discards or omits every-thing about religion, except a very little which he distorts or misrepresents. I think that History should not only be pleasant and authentic, as Critics say, but that the Historian should not be entirely cold and incredulous upon the most important topic in every point of view that ever occupied the attention of man.

He came later to doubt this view of Livy. In his essay on History (*Edinburgh*, May 1828), he declared that Livy

> must be considered as forming a class by himself: no historian with whom we are acquainted has shown so complete an indifference to truth. He seems to have cared only about the picturesque effect of his book, and the honour of his country. On the other hand, we do not know, in the whole range of literature, an instance of a bad thing so well done. The painting of the narrative is beyond description vivid and graceful. The abundance of interesting sentiments and splendid imagery in the speeches is almost

miraculous. His mind is a soil which is never over-teemed, a fountain which never seems to trickle.

By 29 May 1835 when he wrote from India to Ellis upon the question, he was looking closer at the sources of that fountain, and dwelling in particular on Perizonius' brilliant guess that the stories of King and the early Republic came from data in lost chronicles themselves assembled from folk tradition chiefly expressed in song. Casual readers of *The Lays of Ancient Rome* assume that it is trying to recreate the worlds of Horatius and Lars Porsena in the first two poems it presents. It is not. It is trying to recreate the world of four anonymous bards singing and, in at least some cases, composing lays based on ancient traditions. The intelligent reader should not expect to discover the world of Achilles and Hector from the *Iliad*: what survived of that world in the *Iliad* was probably small and for the most part impossible of internal deduction. What we do discover from the *Iliad* is the world of Homer, or at least the forms of cultural identification held by himself and his audience.[49]

So Macaulay created four dream bards. He is very firm that their purpose was didactic. All were using their narratives for certain effects, each different from the others. He wanted to ensure also that the changes in the Rome where they sang became clear, both in the occasion of the songs and in the cultural frames of reference employed in them. He had played with anonymous singers before, when at twenty-three he wrote his songs of the French and English Civil Wars (the exception to anonymity being his Puritan Serjeant in Ireton's regiment at Naseby whom he named Obadiah Bind-their-Kings-in-Chains-and-their-Nobles-with-Links-of-Iron), but although we get a strong impression of them their concern is with the present and the immediate past, so immediate that the bards of Ivry and Naseby imagine themselves to be going through the ordeal of battle once more. But in the *Lays* he was looking at the impact of the remote past on the present, on the means that were used to harness it for present-day purposes, and on the way in which its cultivation offered hearers a kind of super-ego.

The first bard is a plebeian Tory. Of the four he is far the most lovable, and much the most personal. (It seems possible that Macaulay had Samuel Johnson in mind.) The social views of the 'Virginia' bard and the imperial views of the 'Capys' bard are much more fully expressed for much more tangible purposes, but they are not private poems; nor is the ceremonial 'Lake Regillus' private. 'Horatius' alone is described as being 'made' rather than 'sung' in such-and-such-a-year. It ends with what looks like a description of its own rendition, in a family context, as the Macaulays used to hear Tom's compositions. But apart from this, which would derive in part from the early draft of 'Horatius' being written so soon after Margaret's death, the idea conveys a smaller Rome than is present as background to any of the later lays. It is also a Rome showing no sign of the cultural Hellenization which so deeply affects the bard of 'Lake Regillus'. Macaulay wrote in his head-note:

> The author seems to have been an honest citizen, proud of the military glory of his country, sick of the disputes of factions, and much given to pining after good old times which had never really existed. The allusion, however, to the partial manner in which the public lands were allotted, could proceed only from a plebeian....

In other words, the bard is apparently as antithetical to Macaulay's own views as could be imagined, apart from a common enthusiasm for patriotic military glory. The voice of the narrator may be best imagined with a Cockney tinge, which indeed had some common ground with what is known of Macaulay's own accents. The lay commemorates a mythical patrician, whose family Macaulay assumed also had its version of the story:

> Polybius, there is reason to believe, heard the tale recited over the remains of some Consul or Praetor descended from the old Horatian patricians; for he introduces it as a specimen of the narratives with which the Romans were in the habit of embellishing their funeral oratory. It is remarkable that, according to him, Horatius defended the bridge alone, and perished in the waters. According to the chronicles which Livy and Dionysius followed, Horatius had two companions, swam safe to shore, and was loaded with honours and rewards.
>
> ...
>
> It is by no means unlikely that there were two old Roman lays about the defence of the bridge; and that, while the story which Livy has transmitted to us was preferred by the multitude,

the other, which ascribed the whole glory to Horatius alone, may have been the favourite with the Horatian house.

Macaulay's choice of the popular version is noteworthy: a lay for an aristocratic funeral would have obvious points of inspiration among his favourite poets from Homer to Scott. He rightly rated Polybius as a historian far above Livy and Dionysius. But his choice gave him a much better means of conveying the general spirit which he saw in that lost Rome, and it foretold a preoccupation of the *History*. He wanted to write for Everyman, and he rejected any suggestion of servitude to the great aristocratic houses. He had had enough of patronage from Lansdowne and the Hollands. He had been irritated, when writing his essay on Horace Walpole (*Edinburgh*, October 1833), at a sense of obligation to the Hollands which led him to refrain 'from laying a hand' (as he wrote to Hannah on 14 October 1833) 'which has been thought not to be a light one on that old rogue the first Lord Holland'. Much good did his solicitude do him. A month later he had to tell Hannah he found Lady Holland 'in a furious rage at my article on Walpole. ... Lord Holland told me, in an aside, that he quite agreed with me, but that we had better not discuss the subject.' He delivered his belated strictures on Henry Fox, first Lord Holland, in a place where Lady Holland could hardly object to them: the affectionate tribute to her husband he wrote for the *Edinburgh* at her request. When receiving offers of the freedom of aristocratic collections of family papers for use in his *History* he would go out of his way to advise the owners when he thought that his account of their ancestors was likely to be hostile, and was inclined to be over-zealous in guarding his prejudices against contagion by the benevolence of the heirs of his targets: more modern historians sin in the opposite direction. He strongly suspected Livy of having written the Roman victory at the Metaurus over Hannibal's brother Hasdrubal in terms which reflected undue credit on the house of Claudius.[50]

His bard, like himself, was ready enough to give credit to dead patricians where he thought it was their due, and Macaulay stated the supposition of Barthold Georg Niebuhr that 'each of the three defenders of the bridge was the representative of one of the three patrician tribes, is both ingenious and probable, and has been adopted'. But while the bard does not like the factiousness of his fellow plebeians he sympathizes with their grievances, and the archetypal patrician heroes would form a contrast above all to their own greedy descendants:

> And straight against that great array
>   Forth went the dauntless Three.
> For Romans in Rome's quarrel
>   Spared neither land nor gold,
> Nor son nor wife, nor limb nor life,
>   In the brave days of old.
>
> Then none was for a party;
>   Then all were for the state;
> Then the great man helped the poor,
>   And the poor man loved the great:
> Then lands were fairly portioned;
>   Then spoils were fairly sold:
> The Romans were like brothers
>   In the brave days of old.
>
> Now Roman is to Roman
>   More hateful than a foe,
> And the Tribunes beard the high,
>   And the Fathers grind the low.
> As we wax hot in faction,
>   In battle we wax cold:
> Wherefore men fight not as they fought
>   In the brave days of old.

There is contrivance here in the midst of employing the bardic principle of repetition: at the end of the third citation of 'the brave days of old' the poor old narrator seems to be finding the comfort of his myth a little threadbare. But he rescues himself by escaping back to his story while maintaining his moral:

> Now while the Three were tightening
>   Their harness on their backs,
> The Consul was the foremost man
>   To take in hand an axe:
> And Fathers mixed with Commons,
>   Seized hatchet, bar and crow,
> And smote upon the planks above,
>   And loosed the props below.

In the last resort, all have to save the city by taking a common part in a plebeian activity, without which the aristocratic defenders will be making a useless stand. 'Horatius' is not intended as a poem for either social or literary elites.

But it is a poem of plebeian imperialism. In his headnote Macaulay added that 'the poet shared in the general discontent with which the proceedings of Camillus, after the taking of Veii, were regarded': the bard speaks for a people anxious to enrich themselves by exploiting conquered Italian territories. It is this which justifies the exotic account of the Etruscan army at the beginning: the various places of origin of its champions are of interest to the plebeian bard as places which can yield wealth and status to his own people if only the city recovers its military fitness and the booty is fairly apportioned. Nevertheless the poem is at its most intense in its devotion to the city, and suggests a remote origin for the glorification of the name of Rome by future soldiers whose lives may be spent hundreds of miles from it. The initial interest of young Tom in the meaning of lost religions for their societies receives remarkable illustration. 'Horatius' has no trace of cults of gods of Greek origin such as Castor and Pollux, whose celebration a century later provides the occasion for singing 'The Battle of the Lake Regillus'. (At the most crucial moment in 'Lake Regillus' the Hellenized bard reverts, however, and becomes as local in loyalties as the old plebeian of 'Horatius' himself: as the Latins' army breaks the bard bursts out:

> Now, by our Sire Quirinus,
>   It was a goodly sight
> To see the thirty standards
>   Swept down the tide of flight.

Quirinus was a very local god, supposedly brought in by the Sabines assimilated into Rome under Romulus: he was probably a war god, but the details of his cult are part of the lost ancient Rome.) Religion in 'Horatius' relates to the agent of preservation and destruction, the River Tiber, and this at least seems one point where Macaulay was influenced by ancient Indian cults and customs. Primitive worship of the Ganges made it easier for him to convey primitive worship

of the Tiber, which itself acquires an embodiment when it engulfs
the finally demolished bridge:

> And, like a horse unbroken,
>   When first he feels the rein,
> The furious river struggled hard,
>   And tossed his tawny mane,
> And burst the curb, and bounded,
>   Rejoicing to be free,
> And whirling down, in fierce career,
> Battlement, and plank, and pier,
>   Rushed headlong to the sea.
>
> Alone stood brave Horatius,
>   But constant still in mind;
> Thrice thirty thousand foes before,
>   And the broad flood behind.
> 'Down with him!' cried false Sextus
>   With a smile on his pale face.
> 'Now yield thee', cried Lars Porsena,
>   'Now yield thee to our grace.'
>
> Round turned he, as not deigning
>   Those craven ranks to see;
> Nought spake he to Lars Porsena,
>   To Sextus nought spake he;
> But he saw on Palatinus
>   The white porch of his home;
> And he spake to the noble river
>   That rolls by the towers of Rome.
>
> 'Oh, Tiber! father Tiber!
>   To whom the Romans pray,
> A Roman's life, a Roman's arms,
>   Take thou in charge this day!'
> So he spake, and speaking sheathed
>   The good sword by his side,
> And with his harness on his back,
>   Plunged headlong in the tide.

The same theme reappears in 'The Prophecy of Capys'. This lay,
in celebration of the triumph of Manius Curius Dentatus over King

Pyrrhus of Epirus and his fellow Greeks of Tarentum, is stated as
being sung latest in time of all four, but it apparently incorporates
a much earlier ballad. The triumphal bard, once again a plebeian,
is deliberately made boastful, and assumes that the long-ago Capys
would have devoted his lengthiest prophecies to M. Curius Dentatus; but the passages on the wolf seem to have come from a time
of primitive religious outlook when lycanthropic connotations were
much more immediate. Macaulay was in part inspired by Rubens's
painting of the Tiber, the children and the wolf which he had seen
during his visit to Rome. He would have assumed his audience
knew all about the feast of Lupercal and its fertility rite from Shakespeare's *Julius Caesar*, which indicated the long fosterage of the cult.
Nevertheless the introduction in particular makes its associations
in simple form:

> The ravening she-wolf knew them,
>   And licked them o'er and o'er,
> And gave them of her own fierce milk,
>   Rich with raw flesh and gore.
>
> . . .
>
> On the right goes Romulus,
>   With arms to the elbows red,
> And in his hand a broadsword,
>   And on the blade a head —
>
> . . .
>
> On the left side goes Remus,
>   With wrists and fingers red,
> And in his hand a boar-spear,
>   And on the point a head —

Capys then distinguishes Romulus and Rome from those:

> '. . . who of man's seed are born,
>   Whom woman's milk have fed.
> Thou wast not made for lucre,
>   For pleasure, nor for rest;
> Thou, that are sprung from the War-god's loins,
>   And hast tugged at the she-wolf's breast.'

G.K.Chesterton, in the course of *The Victorian Age in Literature* (1913), which includes one of the most illuminating critiques of Macaulay ever written, remarks that for all Macaulay's belief in progress 'he seems to have held that religion can never get any better and that poetry rather tends to get worse'. In his essay on Ranke's *Popes* Macaulay had written:

> It is a mistake to imagine that subtle speculations touching the Divine attributes, the origin of evil, the necessity of human actions, the foundation of moral obligation, imply any high degree of intellectual culture.... The book of Job shows that, long before letters and arts were known to Ionia, these vexing questions were debated with no common skill and eloquence, under the tents of the Idumean Emirs; nor has human reason, in the course of three thousand years, discovered any satisfactory solution of the riddles which perplexed Eliphaz and Zophar.

The wolf and the Tiber are given the opportunity to show their claims on their votaries, and the social implications of those claims. If the cult of the wolf is less attractive than the prayer of Horatius to the Tiber, Capys invests her with a hard dignity which makes the most of her refusal to seek attractiveness:

> 'But thy nurse will hear no master;
>   Thy nurse will bear no load;
> And woe to them that shear her,
>   And woe to them that goad!
> When all the pack, loud baying,
>   Her bloody lair surrounds,
> She dies in silence, biting hard,
>   Amidst the dying hounds.'

Macaulay's essay on Dryden (*Edinburgh*, January 1828) began with a discussion of the origin of imaginative writing:

> The first works of the imagination are... poor and rude, not from the want of genius, but from the want of materials....
>   Yet the effect of these early performances, imperfect as they must necessarily be, is immense. All deficiencies are supplied by

the susceptibility of those to whom they are addressed. We all know what pleasure a wooden doll, which may be bought for sixpence, will afford to a little girl. She will require no other company. She will nurse it, dress it, and talk to it all day.... In the same manner, savages are more affected by the rude compositions of their bards than nations more advanced in civilisation by the greatest master-pieces of poetry.

In process of time, the instruments by which the imagination works are brought to perfection. Men have not more imagination than their rude ancestors. We strongly suspect that they have much less. But they produce better works of imagination. Thus, up to a certain period, the diminution of the poetical powers is far more than compensated by the improvement of all the appliances and means of which those powers stand in need. Then comes the short period of splendid and consummate excellence. And then, from causes against which it is vain to struggle, poetry begins to decline. The progress of language, which was at first favourable, becomes fatal to it, and, instead of compensating for the decay of the imagination, accelerates that decay, and renders it more obvious....

What Macaulay was therefore seeking to do was somehow to reach the state of simplicity of religion and poetry of the earliest Roman time. He did not make, though he could have made, the claim for 'The Prophecy of Capys' that it enshrined material from a far earlier age, preserved by folk tradition with its long fidelity to ancient forms amid the newer sophistication of a Hellenizing culture which was first to prettify and then to destroy it. The Greek conflict with Rome enabled the lay of Capys to offer a fine opposition: the memory of the age of the wolf encountered the reality of the age of the elephant:

'The Greek shall come against thee,
    The conqueror of the East,
Beside him stalks to battle
    The huge earth-shaking beast,
The beast on whom the castle
    With all its guards doth stand,
The beast who hath between his eyes
    The serpent for a hand.'

The terror of Pyrrhus' new form of warfare seems to be throwing the Roman bard to find renewal of strength in the invocation of Rome's ancient ally in the animal kingdom. Some whiff of primitive fear of the elephant is realized in terms which may be very similar to those with which the horrified Romans looked their first at the unearthly thing embattled against them.[51]

Macaulay in the *Lays* drew explicitly on one Scottish source, implicitly on another. He specifically cited Scott, 'who united to the fire of a great poet the minute curiosity and patient diligence of a great antiquary', hailed his achievement in saving the relics of Border minstrelsy, and even mentioned *The Lay of the Last Minstrel* in a footnote to a line in 'Horatius' itself. The Highlands featured only in a *tour d'horizon* to show the universal character of ballad traditions: the Germans, the Gauls, the Saxons, the Danes, the Welsh, the Servians, the Incas, the Azerbaijanis, the Sandwich Islanders, the central Africans, the Castilians and above all the ancient Greeks. But the allusion is significant: 'In the Highlands of Scotland may still be gleaned some relics of the old songs about Cathullin and Fingal.' He had to be circumspect: the great success of Macpherson's *Ossian* throughout Europe was now known to have been founded on forgery and misrepresentation, and Macaulay was anxious to avoid appearing to endorse what he would probably have regarded as the prime fraud of the previous century. But Macpherson had initially based himself on existing ancient heroic poems, to which Scott alludes in *The Antiquary* and which Macaulay cites here. What Macaulay did not say was that the Celtic bardic tradition meant a great deal more to him than that. His *History*, when discussing the Highlands, could be more open, although he was careful to say nothing about family tradition for lengthy descriptions of Highland society going far beyond the printed sources he cited. He showed a mastery of sanguinary legend which indicates preoccupations analogous to those of the bard of 'Capys'. He made great claims for the Gaelic intellectuals:

> It is probable that, in the Highland councils, men who would not have been qualified for the duty of parish clerks sometimes argued questions of peace and war, of tribute and homage, with ability worthy of Halifax and Caermarthen, and that, at the Highland banquets, minstrels who did not know their letters sometimes poured forth rhapsodies in which a discerning critic might

have found passages such as would have reminded him of the tenderness of Otway or of the vigour of Dryden.

This may have been the result, in part, of his father's account of his bardic namesake. It certainly seems impossible to think of any source other than his family for its judiciously worded confidence, a confidence very different from the crassness with which he occasionally discoursed on matters with which his acquaintance was superficial. The point was a matter of personal credentials for him, in an increasingly racialist cultural climate. The next sentence is: 'There was therefore even then evidence sufficient to justify the belief that no natural inferiority had kept the Celt far behind the Saxon.' The figure of a Gaelic bard haunts other passages. In describing the massacre of Glencoe he concludes:

> When the troops had retired, the Macdonalds crept out of the caverns of Glencoe, ventured back to the spot where the huts had formerly stood, collected the scorched corpses from among the smoking ruins, and performed some rude rites of sepulture. The tradition runs that the hereditary bard of the tribe took his seat on a rock which overhung the place of slaughter, and poured forth a long lament over his murdered brethren and his desolate home. Eighty years later that sad dirge was still repeated by the population of the valley.

In the preface to the *Lays* he says of the ballad tradition:

> it reached its full prefection in ancient Greece; for there can be no doubt that the great Homeric poems are generally ballads, though widely distinguished from all other ballads, and indeed from almost all other human compositions, by transcendent sublimity and beauty.

And he saw Highland society as providing material for a Homer. His *History* concludes its description of Cameron of Lochiel (owing too much, as he could not know, to the improvement of Lochiel's memoirs by a descendant):

> In truth, the character of this great chief was depicted two thousand five hundred years before his birth, and depicted – such

is the power of genius – in colours which will be fresh as many years after his death. He was the Ulysses of the Highlands.

Or again:

A Highland bard might easily have found in the history of the year 1689 subjects very similar to those with which the war of Troy furnished the great poets of antiquity. One day Achilles is sullen, keeps his tent, and announces his intention to depart with all his men. The next day Ajax is storming about the camp, and threatening to cut the throat of Ulysses.[52]

The idea of the bard in Macaulay's mind, outside of any family information given him about the elder Zachary Macaulay and others, took its shape from Thomas Gray's 'The Bard', with its poetic encapsulation of English history prophesying doom on the Plantagenets and triumph for the Tudors. The seer Capys owes something to Gray's bard, although his prophecy of future history is in praise of Romulus where Gray's bard curses Edward I. But Matthew Arnold also loved Gray's poem, and went shouting around Wales: 'Hear from the grave, great Taliesin, hear!' Why their divergence?[53]

Macaulay gives us the clue in a curious passage of the *History* about the arrival of Alexander Robertson of Struan to join the Jacobite forces after Killiecrankie. Struan's support had no influence on subsequent events as he described them.

His part, however, in public affairs was so insignificant that his name would not now be remembered, if he had not left a volume of poems, always very stupid and often very profligate. Had this book been manufactured in Grub Street, it would scarcely have been honoured with a quarter of a line in the Dunciad. But it attracted some notice on account of the situation of the writer. For, a hundred and twenty years ago, an eclogue or a lampoon written by a Highland chief was a literary portent.

It portended the ultimate triumph of Celtic literature *in English*. Gray's poem makes just such an assertion, apart from being in English itself: his bard specifically proclaims Spenser, Shakespeare and Milton as his heirs. Moreover Gray's poem was a form of English historical narrative, spanning three centuries. Macaulay was casting himself for just such an inheritance. He was to continue in English the work of Celtic bards, as Gray had declared the great English poets had done. Some of Arnold's anger against Macaulay arose from the elder man's indifference to the collection of Celtic manuscripts by governmental archives. To Macaulay the activity was pernicious. It held back the people of his paternal ancestors from realizing their true place in English society. His passage on the Celt's non-inferiority to the Saxon in the *History* continues:

> It might safely have been predicted that, if ever an efficient police should make it impossible for the Highlander to avenge his wrongs by violence and to supply his wants by rapine, if ever his faculties should be developed by the civilising influence of the Protestant religion and of the English language, if ever he should transfer to his country and to her lawful magistrates the affection and respect with which he had been taught to regard his own petty community and his own petty prince, the kingdom would obtain an immense accession of strength for all the purposes both of peace and of war.

He himself was the proof of that. He had not even permitted himself to become the creature of a valuable and influential political patron, for all of the munificence of Lord Lansdowne (whose family name was Petty-Fitzmaurice). As for the great bards, they had flourished in a world of illiteracy, their great strength had been in oral declamation; any attempt at the transcription of their magnificent compositions would in Macaulay's view result in the saving of the weakest, or in their becoming the prey of exploiters such as James Macpherson. The nature of human progress must destroy any possibility of recreating their achievement, unless it would be possible for some extraordinary person to re-enter their time. To do so that person must begin by trying his hand at bardic work in its own right, but in his own tongue: *The Lays of Ancient Rome*. And then he was ready for his epic. What Struan's poems had portended above all was the last of the great bardic achievements, Macaulay's *History of England*.[54]

Considered in this light, *The Lays of Ancient Rome* assumes a new character. It is in its way a conscious attempt to follow the practice of his master, Scott, in presenting romantic material orchestrated with scientific intent and profound scholarship. But it was not so easy to keep the material from dominating its master at all times. Chesterton observed that 'There were two Macaulays, a rational Macaulay who was generally wrong, and a romantic Macaulay who was almost invariably right.' Macaulay might saddle and bridle Pegasus, but Pegasus sometimes took him to very strange places. Chesterton, could we consult him, would find the rational Macaulay in the importance of Protestantizing the Highlands and the romantic Macaulay in the tears at *Stabat Mater*. It is one thing to create a highly probable nostalgic plebeian bard, announce that his cult of antiquity is founded on nothing, and write a lengthy passage at the conclusion of the third chapter of the *History* on the delusion that leads people to overestimate the happiness of previous generations; it is another to make 'the brave days of old' an undying phrase in the language. It is one thing to praise the improvement of the Highlands; it is another to provide a portrait of the great architect of a design for their improvement, the Master of Stair, which relentlessly traces his ideological conviction to an outcome in the Massacre of Glencoe. Macaulay's attractiveness – and indeed his value – in part flow from his inability to silence within himself the lament for poetry murdered by progress.[55]

The Lays of Ancient Rome offered four bardic voices (and, in 'The Prophecy of Capys', a shadowy fifth who must have supplied the original version of the story on which centuries later its noisy chauvinist narrator drew); none of these voices was intended to be Macaulay's. Occasionally he employed ironies of the kind he had used in 'Ivry': the chauvinism of the reciter of 'Capys' invites reservation especially in its contempt for the people of Tarentum, which contrasts conspicuously with the respect shown to the enemy in 'Horatius' and 'Lake Regillus'. In 'Horatius' the example is justly famous:

> No sound of joy or sorrow
>   Was heard from either bank;
> But friends and foes in dumb surprise,
> With parted lips and straining eyes,
>   Stood gazing where he sank;
> And when above the surges
>   They saw his crest appear,
> All Rome sent forth a rapturous cry

> And even the ranks of Tuscany
> Could scarce forbear to cheer.

In 'Lake Regillus' the Homeric influence (which Macaulay insisted was present in the original myth, thus distinguishing it from the legends of the war against Porsena) carried some of the Homeric objectivity: several of the enemy are heroic, including the Prince Mamilius (and his horse), and Titus 'the youngest Tarquin,/Too good for such a breed'. The 'Capys' narrator seems petty and vengeful by comparison. The withdrawal of sympathy from him was perhaps the reverse of the mood in which the Secretary-at-War had bade defiance to the pretensions of China. Macaulay in verse showed depths of sympathy for figures who might be expected to win the scorn of Macaulay in prose. 'Lake Regillus' included the death of a Roman exile, Julius

> Of Rome's great Julian line;
> Julius, who left his mansion
> High on the Velian hill,
> And through all turns of weal and woe
> Followed proud Tarquin still.
> Now right across proud Tarquin
> A corpse was Julius laid....

Macaulay returned to the idea in his most sensitive poem, 'Epitaph of a Jacobite', conceived in whole-hearted sorrow for the sacrifices of an English follower of James II in exile.[56]

'Lake Regillus' is a highly official poem, the bard making the commemoration of Castor and Pollux at their feast. Macaulay had gone to considerable trouble to research that event. But his making it so official gives a slight note of irony of its own. This narrator is a Roman anticipation of a British Poet Laureate, and Macaulay saw little good in that office in his own day. Governmental subvention was to him as degrading as any other form of patronage, as he had asserted in his youth in *Knight's* when denouncing the competition system of the Royal Society of Literature. He thought the history of the Poet Laureates involved such worthless figures that the office should be abolished, but characteristically drew back from his own principle to advocate (unsuccessfully) the claim of James Henry Leigh Hunt on the ground that he needed the money. It therefore amused him to make the most Laureate-like poem the most absurd, in its parachuting of imaginary gods into battle-narrative.[57]

The bard of 'Virginia' raises a different question. Officially Macaulay would have disapproved of him. The lay is a vicious personal attack on one of the enemies of the plebeian popular leaders in the aftermath of their successful re-election as tribunes, and by making the most of the loathsome reputation (among plebeians) of the grandfather of that enemy, Appius Claudius Crassus, the narrator virtually incites the crowd to riot against him by reminding them of what their ancestors did to his:

> One stone hit Appius in the mouth, and one beneath the ear;
> And ere he reached Mount Palatine, he swooned with pain and
>   fear.
> His cursed head, that he was wont to hold so high with pride,
> Now, like a drunken man's, hung down, and swayed from side
>   to side;
> And when his stout retainers had brought him to his door,
> His face and neck were all one cake of filth and clotted gore.
> As Appius Claudius was that day, so may his grandson be!
> God send Rome one such other sight, and send me there to see!

It seemed to foretell the mob rule Macaulay found so hateful in the French Revolution. On the other hand, it was his business as he saw it to relate the enthusiasms and manners probable among his putative bards whatever his preferences: as he said, the coarse boasts put in the mouth of Capys by his bard were analogous to those Virgil makes the dead Anchises utter in the Sixth Book of the *Aeneid*. He wanted to portray a culture which he believed to resemble his view of Highland society in its vindictiveness in hereditary feud. But there was a source for the poem in his own political experience, and one much less tangential than possible secret doubts about the Opium War or about British state ceremonies of dubious archaic origin analogous to the festival rejoicings for which 'Lake Regillus' was composed. In his headnote to 'Virginia', Macaulay stated that the plebeians' 'position bore some resemblance to that of the Irish Catholics during the interval between the year 1792 and the year 1829'. His own observation of Daniel O'Connell in Parliament would therefore have informed both the general tone

he gave his bard and the speech within the lay when the young
Icilius makes his impassioned protest at the attempt of Appius Claudius the elder to gain legal custody of the person of Virginia.

'Exult, ye proud Patricians! The hard-fought fight is o'er.
We strove for honours – 'twas in vain: for freedom – 'tis no
    more.

. . .

Still, like a spreading ulcer, which leech-craft may not cure,
Let your foul usance eat away the substance of the poor.
Still let your haggard debtors bear all their fathers bore;
Still let your dens of torment be noisome as of yore;
No fire when Tiber freezes; no air in dog-star heat;
And store of rods for free-born backs, and holes for free-born
    feet.
Heap heavier still the fetters; bar closer still the grate;
Patient as sheep we yield us up unto your cruel hate.
But, by the Shades beneath us, and by the Gods above,
Add not unto your cruel hate your yet more cruel love!
Have ye not graceful ladies, whose spotless lineage springs
From Consuls, and High Pontiffs, and ancient Alban kings?
Ladies, who deign not on our paths to set their tender feet,
Who from their cars look down with scorn upon the wondering
    street,
Who in Corinthian mirrors their own proud smile behold,
And breathe of Capuan odours, and shine with Spanish gold?
Then leave the poor Plebeian his single tie to life –
The sweet, sweet love of daughter, of sister, and of wife,
The gentle speech, the balm for all that his vexed soul endures,
The kiss, in which he half forgets even such a yoke as yours.
Still let the maiden's beauty swell the father's breast with pride;
Still let the bridegroom's arms enfold an unpolluted bride.
Spare us the inexpiable wrong, the unutterable shame,
That turns the coward's heart to steel, the sluggard's blood to
    flame,
Lest, when our latest hope is fled, ye taste of our despair,
And learn by proof, in some wild hour, how much the wretched
    dare.'

Livy and Dionysius mention a speech by Icilius, but give him the motive of marital engagement to Virginia with a male chauvinist insistence on his right to her virginity: Macaulay makes him an altruistic spokesman for his people among whom it has previously been established that Virginia is a universal favourite child (it is a particularly chilling point that Appius Claudius is apparently the first person to realize she has become a woman). Macaulay was not in Parliament before Catholic Emancipation and therefore made no speeches on it that have come down to us, but his satires in verse against the High Tories show the passion of his feeling and his identification with the Irish Catholics in the racial antipathy which lay behind opposition to their admission to Parliament. But where Icilius is describing his people's wrongs, Irish-style, as an argument for alienation, the bard of 'Virginia' would have resembled Macaulay in seeking to use the past as a means of integration. The bard has seen the defeat, and hopes he will see the destruction, of Appius Claudius the younger. Future plebeians may make terms with some patricians – there is a hint of it from the bard:

> Though the great houses love us not, we own, to do them right,
> That the great houses, all save one, have borne them well in
> fight.
> Still Caius of Corioli, his triumphs and his wrongs,
> His vengeance and his mercy, live in our camp-fire songs.
> Beneath the yoke of Furius oft have Gaul and Tuscan bowed;
> And Rome may bear the pride of him of whom herself is proud.
> But evermore a Claudius shrinks from a stricken field,
> And changes colour like a maid at sight of sword and shield.
> The Claudian triumphs all were won within the city towers;
> The Claudian yoke was never pressed on any necks but ours.
> A Cossus, like a wild cat, springs ever at the face;
> A Fabius rushes like a boar against the shouting chase;
> But the vile Claudian litter, raging with currish spite,
> Still yelps and snaps at those who run, still runs from those who
> smite.

And Macaulay was a member of the Melbourne ministry allied with O'Connell. Before he had gone to India, and before that alliance had been forged, he had spoken in the Commons against O'Connell's motion for the repeal of the Union (later tacitly dropped by the Irish leader during his Whig alliance): 'Calumny, abuse, royal displeasure, popular fury, exclusion from office, exclusion from Parliament, we were ready to endure them all, rather than that he should be less than a British subject. We never will suffer him to be more.' His *History* tried to grapple with the same question: how far the Irish absorption in the past could be made the means for spurring forward Irish integration and participation in 'England'.[58]

'Virginia' is also an intensely personal poem, and in its climax especially reflects Macaulay's horror at the idea of any man possessing his sisters Hannah and Margaret. When Virginius' fatherhood of his daughter has been successfully if unjustly called into question by Appius Claudius, he tells her:

> '... See how he points his eager hand this way!
> See how his eyes gloat on thy grief, like a kite's upon the prey!
> With all his wit, he little deems, that, spurned, betrayed, bereft,
> Thy father hath in his despair one fearful refuge left.
> He little deems that in this hand I clutch what still can save
> Thy gentle youth from taunts and blows, the portion of the slave;
> Yea, and from nameless evil, that passeth taunt and blow –
> Foul outrage which thou knowest not, which thou shalt never
>   know.
> Then clasp me round the neck once more, and give me one more
>   kiss;
> And now, mine own dear little girl, there is no way but this.'
> With that, he lifted high the steel, and smote her in the side,
> And in her blood she sank to earth, and with one sob she died.

The same motives are those which animate Horatius:

> 'And how can man die better
>   Than facing fearful odds,
> For the ashes of his fathers,
>   And the temples of his Gods,
>
> And for the tender mother
>   Who dandled him to rest,
> And for the wife who nurses
>   His baby at her breast,
> And for the holy maidens

> Who feed the eternal flame,
> To keep them from false Sextus
> That wrought the deed of shame ?'

W. W. Robson has remarked on the chilling assumption of Virginius that his daughter's opinions on her own survival are never to be asked at all. There is a terrible irony in poor Leslie Stephen restricting *The Lays of Ancient Rome* to 'swing and fire', on which he compliments Macaulay, while denying his poetry the 'far higher quality which Macaulay could not do at all'; in the years when he wrote about Macaulay for the *Cornhill* (and in his DNB), he gave the name Virginia to a child who would exhibit him in *To the Lighthouse* (when she had become Virginia Woolf) as a father supremely indifferent to the emotions of his own children. Her life would also ultimately and violently be taken by a human agency, her own. The death of Virginia meant more to Macaulay than he could admit; did it also mean more to Stephen than he could admit ?[59]

Macaulay's idea of a society finding its greatest expression of literary identity in the defence of women against sexual attack produced remarkable poetry because it related so closely to his own tragedy; feminist critique of it would presumably cut two ways, condemning a paternalism repressive to the point of sickness while acknowledging the wisdom of its priorities in seeing women so much at risk from male predators. In any case, it made an excellent historical point on the organization and self-expression of primitive societies, and it accords with the advantages and perils of his own time-travelling that he recognized much more primitive impulses in ancient Rome than were assumed by the scholars and teachers of his own time. He ran the risk of making Virginius a Victorian exemplar. The Victorian paterfamilias may not be thought of as a plebeian; but much of the middle-class majority of Macaulay's audience had come from plebeian roots and won their social place against aristocratic defences. Macaulay was not seeking to make Virginius a Victorian, and went to some lengths in his preface and headnotes to emphasize the contrasts between ancient Roman and modern British ethics; but it was the verse, not the notes, which was adopted. Similarly, while the intent of the imperial boasting in 'The Prophecy of Capys' is partly to invite reader's irony, much of what Macaulay singled out as characteristic of the old Roman bards became the stock-in-trade of their mid-Victorian successors: 'the illiberal sneers at the Greeks, the furious party-spirit, the contempt for the arts of peace, the love of war for its own sake, the ungenerous exultation over the vanquished'. It is not that he was a Philistine, but that the Philistines refashioned what he brought them into their own images and likenesses. Macaulay was only the apostle to the Philistines.[60]

3 The Essays relating to history

> It may be laid down as a general rule, though subject
> to considerable qualifications and exceptions, that his-
> tory begins in novel and ends in essay.
>
> Macaulay, 'History',
> *Edinburgh Review* (May 1828)

When Macaulay published what he called *Critical and Historical Essays Contributed to the Edinburgh Review* in 1843, he thereby prompted distinctions between his adjectives from future commentators and anthologists, but there was no such clear distinction in his own mind. He would have agreed that his essay on Robert Montgomery's poems (*Edinburgh*, April 1830) was critical, indeed very critical, and that the last essay written for the *Edinburgh* (included in editions of his collection subsequent to its *Edinburgh* appearance in October 1844) made no allusion at all to the books it was ostensibly reviewing, simply moved into discussion of the elder Pitt from the point at which he had broken off in his last Pitt essay, and was clearly historical. But none of the essays was to be seen as wholly free from either quality. The public occasion for the onslaught on Montgomery was a denunciation of the practice of 'puffing' and the means by which the reputations of worthless writers were inflated, but this necessitated a brief sketch of the decline of literary patronage and the growth of market dependence; the more private occasion was that Montgomery was a vigorous Tory, much inclined to make his contribution to scaremongering against Reform by dark discussion of the French Revolution; the most private occasion was that Montgomery had written a scurrilous attack on Zachary Macaulay, James Stephen and the apostles of anti-slavery, on which Tom Macaulay said nothing at all. The historical element in answering Montgomery on the French Revolution was ostensibly small, but its subtext was immense. Macaulay was quoting from Montgomery's *The Omnipresence of the Deity*:

And here let Memory turn her tearful glance
On the dark horrors of tumultuous France,
When blood and blasphemy defiled her land,
And fierce Rebellion shook her savage hand.

Whether Rebellion shakes her own hand, shakes the hand of
Memory, or shakes the hand of France, or what any one of these
three metapors would mean, we know no more than we know
what is the sense of the following passage:

Let the foul orgies of infuriate crime
Picture the raging havoc of that time,
When leagued Rebellion march'd to kindle man,
Fright in her rear, and Murder in her van.
And thou, sweet flower of Austria, slaughter'd Queen,
Who dropp'd no tear upon the dreadful scene,
When gush'd the life-blood from thine angel form,
And martyr'd beauty perish'd in the storm,
Once worshipp'd paragon of all who saw,
Thy look obedience, and thy smile a law.

What is the distinction between the foul orgies and the raging
havoc which the foul orgies are to picture? Why does Fright
go behind Rebellion, and Murder before? Why should not Murder fall behind Fright? Or why should not all the three walk
abreast? We have read of a hero who had

Amazement in his van, with flight combined,
And Sorrow's faded form, and Solitude behind.

Gray, we suspect, could have given a reason for disposing the
allegorical attendants of Edward thus. But to proceed. 'Flower
of Austria' is stolen from Byron. 'Dropp'd' is false English. 'Perish'd in the storm' means nothing at all; and 'thy look obedience'
means the very reverse of what Mr Robert Montgomery intends
to say.[61]

On the surface it seems only reiteration of the many other dissec-
tions of Montgomery in the essay, with its charges of ill-fitting pla-
giarisms and pointless personification, and its revelations of the
ludicrous from analysis of metaphors. It was certainly subordinate
to the overall theme of the decay of critical standards in the contagion of a puffery, theme to climax in the Johnsonian roar:

And this is fine poetry! This is what ranks its writer with the master-spirits of the age! This is what has been described, over and over again, in terms which would require some qualification if used respecting Paradise Lost! It is too much that this patch-work, made by stitching together old odds and ends of what, when new, was but tawdry frippery, is to be picked up off the dunghill on which it ought to rot, and to be held up to admiration as an inestimable specimen of art. And what must we think of a system by means of which verses like those we have quoted, verses fit only to form the poet's corner of the Morning Post, can produce emolument and fame? The circulation of this writer's poetry has been greater than that of Southey's Roderick, and beyond all comparison greater than that of Cary's Dante or of the best works of Coleridge.

Macaulay was careful to distinguish between worthless Tory writing such as Montgomery's, and fine Tory writing such as one of his own favourites by Southey (whose Colloquies on Society he had reviewed with high sarcasm in the previous Edinburgh). But he was also improving the shining hour by making nonsense of the Tories' red scare. The martyr-cult of Marie Antoinette went back to a famous passage of Burke; Macaulay was gleefully leaping on the opportunity to take so emotive a memory out of his opponents' armoury by making its promiscuous use so memorably absurd. It is a cunning use of comedy and lampoon to break the Burkean enchantment as part of his lifelong work to reclaim Burke for the cause of civil and religious liberty and Parliamentary sovereignty. In his earlier essay on Milton he had spoken of the need 'to spell the charm backward', in the context of the mystique of Royalism and its attendant repressions: he now literally did so to undo the sentimental force of Royalist legend in the French Revolutionary context where it was used to justify enmity to Catholic Emancipation and Parliamentary reform. He captured the sorcerer by showing his magic destroy itself and its objective in the hands of the sorcerer's apprentice. The brutal ticking off of Montgomery's errors, as if he were a tradesman, was the more deliberate as he intended his efforts to result in the transfer of power to tradesmen. Macaulay was one of the first historians to use the verse and stage satires and lampoons of former ages as historical sources; he did so in part because in their authors he recognized his literary kin.[62]

The word 'critical' was no more intended to be eliminated from the purely historical essays than 'historical' from those that were socio-political or literary. Macaulay as a Greek scholar read many English words in their original meaning: instinctively he saw 'critical' as 'performing the work of a judge'. The *Edinburgh* was a means of furthering popular information and a *journal de combat*. Macaulay saw his business as description and assessment of the several achievements of past historical figures, in the totality and in individual components. His audience expected strong, hortatory views. His own work was one of reclaiming much of the British heritage which Whigs had written off or Tories had arrogated to themselves. For all of his powers of critical demolition he was much more concerned to see the strengths and value of much of what he discussed than earlier scribes in the *Edinburgh* had done. The reason is simple: he was writing for a Whig ideological journal, but he was a complex of more ideologies than the Whig. His style, so startling to Jeffrey, with its great obligations to the Authorised Version and the plays of Shakespeare (hence his phenomenal success in the United States, where he seems to have been the third choice with these two in many households), has as its counterpart his Evangelical method of persuasion, formed from his discussions with Zachary. Even when he was preaching pure Whig doctrine he might, like his father, show hopes of salvation for adversaries. On many occasions he did not forbear to cheer for the ranks of Tuscany.

Modern historical scholarship disapproves of the historian's being a judge; but since Macaulay developed his historical writing in essays he also intended as critical, we should try to understand what this entailed rather than swiftly embark on the somewhat 'Whig' exercise of condemning him by the standards of subsequent generations. One aspect of the critical approach to historical questions was an aesthetic one. Officially Macaulay had his own standards of taste in judgment of historical persons and events. In fact he was highly aware of differences in taste and sought to develop his argument to allow for its influence on minds of a different persuasion from his own. His essay on Barère (*Edinburgh*, April 1844) is an almost unrelieved portrait in human vileness (which seems to have been his reason for excluding it from his *Critical and Historical Essays* when adding later items to subsequent editions); but he was anxious to make it clear that his hatred of Barère could reasonably be shared by persons of more affection for leaders of the French Revolution than himself:

> The genius, courage, patriotism, and humanity of the Girondist statesmen more than atoned for what was culpable in their conduct.... Danton and Robespierre were indeed bad men; but in both of them some important parts of the mind remained sound. Danton was brave and resolute, fond of pleasure, of power, and of distinction, with vehement passions, with lax principles, but with some kind and manly feelings, capable of great crimes, but capable also of friendship and of compassion. He, therefore, naturally finds admirers among persons of bold and sanguine dispositions. Robespierre was a vain, envious and suspicious man, with a hard heart, weak nerves, and a gloomy temper. But we cannot with truth deny that he was, in the vulgar sense of the word, disinterested, that his private life was correct, or that he was sincerely zealous for his own system of politics and morals. He, therefore, naturally finds admirers among honest but moody and bitter democrats.

This kind of perception lies below his formal judgments: he always intended his audience to consist of potential converts as well as Whig votaries, and to it he sought to mean more than he appeared to be saying.[63]

He also on occasion meant less than he appeared to be saying. The sense of a bardic legacy seems to have been with him in writing from an early age – consider the natural reference to Gray's 'The Bard' slipped into his critique of Montgomery on the French Revolution – and his bardic strain inspired him to hyperbole. For instance, he wished to say that the Rev. G.R.Gleig's *Memoirs of the Life of Warren Hastings* from time to time sought to justify Hastings's conduct on the most dubious ethics of pragmatism. This became (*Edinburgh*, October 1841):

> It is not too much to say that Mr Gleig has written several passages, which bear the same relation to the Prince of Machiavelli that the Prince of Machiavelli bears to the Whole Duty of Man, and which would excite amazement in a den of robbers, or on board of a schooner of pirates.

Here Macaulay deliberately intends the reader to fall into giggles at the thought of a Morgan or Blackbeard instructing their interested crews where Mr Gleig had gone too far this time: his purpose is simply to compel attention to an excess of biographical defence advocacy. Or let us take his desire to pay tribute to Pope Benedict XIV, partly in contrast to his successor. This becomes (*Edinburgh*, April 1842): 'Benedict the Fourteenth, the best and wisest of the two hundred and fifty successors of St Peter, was no more.' Macaulay did not mean that he had made full and certain analysis of the morality and intellect of all 250 popes, many of whom are only known to history in the vaguest outline. He meant that he thought Benedict an exceptionally good and wise man. He assumed that his audience would so understand him. As we have seen, he might have had difficulties in defending his proposition on Benedict against his estimate of Nicholas V. But the hyperbole is not carelessness: it has the bardic desire to arouse attention by a powerful turn of descriptive phrase. It is also the mock-heroic in criticism: from the time of his Swift-like journal-letters to Hannah and Margaret in the early 1830s, Macaulay had developed a vein of exuberant self-mockery which returned from 1838 onward as a form of critical style for the amusement of his *Edinburgh* audience, having nowhere else to go. But his wider audience did not always have the insights of Margaret. (Hannah remained an important audience, but she was 'Hannah' now, no longer 'Nancy', and her days as a playfellow in his literary games were over: she seems to have adopted some of the rigidity of her husband, Sir Charles Trevelyan, who would be caricatured by Trollope in *The Three Clerks* as Sir Gregory Hardlines.) Some readers did understand: P.G.Wodehouse makes constructive use of the device.[64]

The chief blend of the critical and the historical in the *Essays* was that at bottom Macaulay saw no real distinction between literary and historical subjects, at least none when he was in his seven-league-booted stride, or when Pegasus was whirling him aloft. Stone-cold, and writing to Macvey Napier, he was nervous about literary criticism: to the world he was a 'bonnie fechter', but to his editor (at least by 26 June 1838 after a nine-year partnership) he opened his self-doubt: 'I am not successful in analyzing the effect of works of genius.... I have never written a page of criticism on poetry or the fine arts which I would not burn if I had the power.... I have a strong and acute enjoyment of great works of the imagination; but I have never habituated myself to dissect them.' These words are those of a great literary critic.

He began his *Edinburgh* work in literary criticism by grounding his comparison of Milton and Dante in the history of their times, and he ended it soon after his establishment of the literary genius of Fanny Burney (January 1843):

> She first showed that a tale might be written in which both the fashionable and the vulgar life of London might be exhibited with great force, and with broad comic humour, and which yet should not contain a single line inconsistent with rigid morality, or even with virgin delicacy. She took away the reproach which lay on a most useful and delightful species of composition. She vindicated the right of her sex to an equal share in a fair and noble province of letters. Several accomplished women have followed in her track. At present, the novels which we owe to English ladies form no small part of the literary glory of our country. No class of works is more honourably distinguished by fine observation, by grace, by delicate wit, by pure moral feeling. Several among the successors... have equalled her; two, we think, have surpassed her. But the fact that she has been surpassed gives her an additional claim to our respect and gratitude; for, in truth, we owe to her not only Evelina, Cecilia, and Camilla, but also Mansfield Park and the Absentee.

This is the close of an essay whose stature as criticism above all consists in making its audience recognize true literary creative power and the advantages and limitations surrounding its owner; and the Parthian shot of driving the just admirers of the genius of Jane Austen and Maria Edgeworth back to pay tribute to Fanny Burney precisely because the latter two are better than she, admirably illustrates the use of the historical sense in literary criticism. (It also illustrates Macaulay's having himself made progress since the slight tendency towards a better-than-Dante critical yardstick in his 'Milton', nearly twenty years earlier.)[65]

But the real point is that there is no frontier in the assessment of cultural achievement by the critic and by the historian. Macaulay's whole life as a historian turned on that. The creative arts, but particularly literature, excited him as the true means by which human achievement in former ages expressed itself at its best, and in which could be studied some of the clearest clues to the nature of former ages. While Macaulay was developing his own ideas on the past, confidently in their self-expression and humbly in their self-estimation, the idea of the 'essay' – an attempt, by definition, without implying finality of judgment – appealed to him as a type of finger-exercise. He was certainly informing his readers in the *Edinburgh* and arming them against their ideological opponents of the hour, but he was also thinking questions through himself with more informality and less assurance than his bold strokes of creative and critical writing imply. Writing to Napier on 18 April 1842 he defended the language of his essay on Frederick the Great (*Edinburgh*, April 1842):

> I certainly should not, in regular history, use some of the phrases which you censure. But I do not consider a review of this sort as regular history.... I would no more use the words *bore* or *awkward squad* in a composition meant to be uniformly serious and earnest then Addison would, in a state-paper, have called Louis an old put....

Nevertheless, if the *History* would be written with more formality, it did not (fortunately) reach the restraint of a state paper, even one by Macaulay. But he was very clear as to the distinction, especially as he was now writing both essays and *History*: 'The tone of many passages, nay of whole pages, would justly be called flippant in a regular history. But I conceive that this sort of composition has its own character and its own laws. I do not claim the honour of having invented it.' Significantly he found literature the means of defining his genre:

> The manner of these little historical essays bears, I think, the same analogy to the manner of Tacitus or Gibbon which... the manner of Shakspeare's historical plays [bears] to the manner of Sophocles.... The despair of Constance in Shakspeare [*King John*] is as lofty as that of Oedipus in Sophocles. But the levities of the bastard Falconbridge would be utterly out of place in Sophocles. Yet we feel that they are not out of place in Shakspeare. So with these historical articles. Where the subject requires it they may rise, if the author can manage it, to the highest altitudes of Thucydides. Then again they may without impropriety sink to the levity and colloquial ease of Horace Walpole's Letters.

This is my theory. – Whether I have succeeded in the execution is quite another question.

He concluded by no more wanting to purge undignified language from his essay 'than I would exclude from such a poem as Don Juan slang terms because such terms would be out of place in Paradise Lost.'[66]

The elements of both epics, *Paradise Lost* and *Don Juan*, would be present in the *History*, and for all of Macaulay's distinction – a distinction often insufficiently stressed – the creative influences he diagnoses in the essays could not easily have been excluded from his own great epic. But, however Byronesque in colloquialism and irony, the essays also hold some epic quality. He went after dramatic and epic effects sometimes in the most obvious of all ways, that of using his exemplars as his sources, as for instance in his assessment of Elizabethan religious loyalties (*Edinburgh*, April 1832):

> The greatest and most popular dramatists of the Elizabethan age ... speak neither like Catholics nor like Protestants, but like persons who are wavering between the two systems, or who have made a system for themselves out of parts selected from both. They seem to hold some of the Romish rites and doctrines in high respect. They treat the vow of celibacy, for example, so tempting, and, in later times, so common a subject for ribaldry, with mysterious reverence. ... The partiality of Shakspeare for Friars is well known. In Hamlet, the Ghost complains that he died without extreme unction, and, in defiance of the article which condemns the doctrine of purgatory, declares that he is
>
>> confined to fast in fires,
>> Till the foul crimes, done in his days of nature,
>> Are burnt and purged away.
>
> These lines, we suspect, would have raised a tremendous storm in the theatre at any time during the reign of Charles the Second. They were clearly not written by a zealous Protestant, or for zealous Protestants. Yet the author of King John and Henry the Eighth was surely no friend to papal supremacy.

Apart from the excellent example in opinion assessment by use of a form of culture so dependent on public approval as the drama, as Macaulay stresses here (and more briefly in the *History*), there is careful management of atmosphere to convey an effect. The Ghost in *Hamlet* gains an additional chill when disclosed as something more than the Ghost we all thought we knew as we shuddered at it, and within it there is a ghost of an unknown and vanished England whose genius could no longer be found represented in any modern religion, Protestant or Catholic. This is not simply to make an argument; it is to allow the past to billow out to the reader in its own terms through its finest form of expression.

Macaulay would do the same thing in using Milton's *Comus* to convey the nature of Milton's own later and larger aims within the Civil War:

> He knew that those who, with the best intentions, overlooked these schemes of reform, and contented themselves with pulling down the King and imprisoning the malignants, acted like the heedless brothers in his own poem, who, in their eagerness to disperse the train of the sorcerer, neglected the means of liberating the captive. They thought only of conquering when they should have thought of disenchanting.

> > 'Oh, ye mistook! Ye should have snatched his wand
> > And bound him fast. Without the rod reversed,
> > And backward mutters of dissevering power,
> > We cannot free the lady that sits here
> > In stony fetters fixed and motionless.'

> To reverse the rod, to spell the charm backward, to break the ties which bound a stupefied people to the seat of enchantment, was the noble aim of Milton. To this all his public conduct was directed.

Formal historical narrative might condemn this use of Milton's early work to shape a view of his mature thought as anachronistic, and certainly Milton had thought that way about Comus before thinking it about Charles, but the fact that his dramatic creation preceded his political thought makes it if anything more important. The creator has a different view of events to the mere participant.

Macaulay's own career was affected by that consideration. His *Essays* gave him informality, intimacy, a measure of freedom from close argument anchored to sources, which made him a bad man to begin learning to wear the shackles of formal historiography in his forties (and the *Lays* had even given him the privilege of choosing the most artistic of several variants with the right of picturesque refinements of his own). Yet as late as 24 June 1842 he was still telling Napier he would not republish his *Edinburgh* essays because of the distinction he saw with the *History*.

> The public judges, and ought to judge, indulgently of periodical works. They not expected to be highly finished. Their natural life is only six weeks. Sometimes the writer is at a distance from the books to which he wants to refer. Sometimes he is forced to hurry through his task in order to catch the post. He may blunder; he may give an immoderate extension to one part of his subject, and dismiss an equally important part in a few words. All this is readily forgiven if there be a certain spirit and vivacity in his style. But as soon as he republishes, he challenges a comparison with all the most symmetrical and polished of human compositions. A painter who has a picture in the exhibition of the Royal Academy would act very unwisely if he took it down and carried it over to the National Gallery. Where it now hangs surrounded by a crowd of daubs which are only once seen and then forgotten, it may pass for a fine piece. He is a fool if he places it side by side with the master-pieces of Titian and Claude.... I will not found any pretensions to the rank of a classic on my reviews. I will remain, according to the excellent precept of the Gospel, at the lower end of the table where I am constantly accosted with 'Friend, go up higher', – and not push my way to the top at the risk of being compelled with shame to take the lowest room. If I live twelve or fifteen years I may perhaps produce something which I may not be afraid to exhibit side by side with the performances of the old masters.

(Napier showed the common sense of the journal he edited in not being offended when Macaulay seemed to be describing its other contributions as 'daubs'. Macaulay had great courtesy, but little tact.)[67]

That Macaulay then took the risk of republishing most of his *Edinburgh* essays narrowed the gap between their original freedom and the formality with which he had conceived his *History*. He won the status of a classic on terms less exacting than he had assumed would be the case, and the effect was to make him over-confident in the judgments he laid down in his *History*. (Again the first, phenomenal, success of the *History* came a little more than six years after that letter to Napier, not the twelve or fifteen he had there ventured to hope.) The identification of Macaulay with the *Critical and Historical Essays*, much more than with *The Lays of Ancient Rome*, tied him to a view of his subject. That at first he got away with the voluptuous style of the *Essays* made for a less austere *History* than might have been the case, but it also imprisoned Macaulay much more in the content of the *Essays* as printed in book form. He might alter specific judgments within the *Essays*, and indeed their close student would find much in which they disagreed with one another – in the character of the statesman and wit George Savile, Marquess of Halifax, for instance, dismissed in an early essay as characteristic of the depraved moral climate of the late seventeenth century, then in subsequent essays steadily receiving more credit, and finally proving the hero of the first part of the *History*. But the ideological contours of the *History* were fairly firmly fixed. Macaulay had not wanted to indicate his disagreements with his former works when he republished them; but now that the *Essays* had the authority of a book, extrication would look like retreat. Ever since his boyhood when his father had worried about his courage, he had not been enthusiastic about retreat. The vast extent of his reading meant that his essays all had some basis in primary research, but it would be hard for the more detailed archival investigation needed for the *History* to free itself from simply supporting and broadening his existing opinions.

Macaulay's essays came fairly late to their preoccupation with primarily historical subjects. His 'Milton' (August 1825) brought in much history arising from its defence of Milton, but it makes it clear that it is Milton himself who elicited its historical interest. His 'Machiavelli' (March 1827) again derived primarily from interest in its subject's own works, though here the historical background assumed a greater concentration in order to explain the origin of the writings. Both essays are a protest against fashionable judgments on a writer which ignore or misread his times and their effect on him, and his effect on them. The essay 'Machiavelli' might seem crude to the point of racism in its dissection of Italian public morality in Machiavelli's time, but in fact Macaulay was to prove as harsh in his depiction of public cynicism under Charles II within a few years. It is also unusual in its efforts to show how much idealism really existed in Machiavelli, how far the cynicism ascribed to him derived from his felicity in the expression of popular ethics, and how much original artistry he possessed, although it sought neither to bring him in as a hero nor to show any sympathy for his political morals as a system. It luxuriated in instructive paradox, and Macaulay was to be attacked as an exponent of paradox for its own sake: but he had early grasped the principle that instruction partly depends on an element of surprise if its lessons are to be memorable. He took this to the happy length of making its corollary into the following general maxim: 'Every man who has seen the world knows that nothing is so useless as a general maxim.' In the cases of both Milton and Machiavelli Macaulay deeply related their stature as writers to their having played so great a part in historical events: if he was to be a writer himself, he seems to be saying, he must reserve his major work until he should have taken a hand in acting history.[68]

We say 'writer' rather than 'historian'. Macaulay was still uncertain as to his preoccupation with history, although history was already furnishing him with innumerable examples in the arguments he wished to formulate in speech or in writing. Apart from an essay on history itself (*Edinburgh*, May 1828), and one on Henry Hallam's *Constitutional History of England* (*Edinburgh*, September 1828), Macaulay's next sixteen essays were on literary, political, social, economic and for the most part contemporary topics. It is striking that his essay on Dryden (*Edinburgh*, January 1828), which he did not reprint in *Critical and Historical Essays*, had much to say on the relative lack of importance of individual men against the tendencies of their ages, on the failure of poetry to survive social sophistication, and on the merits of Dryden's individual compositions, but made almost no contribution to the discussion of English history in Dryden's lifetime – which was also the period covered by the *History*, first published twenty years after. Macaulay made more of the period in his essay on Bunyan, and produced his first detailed discussion of a brief period in history in the same issue of the *Edinburgh* (December 1831) when he wrote on John Hampden and the outbreak of the English Civil War, ending with Hampden's death in 1643. The Hallam essay had followed its subject's chronological limits from 1485 to 1760, but it, too, had given the bulk of its attention to the reign of Charles I. The preoccupation was in keeping with the idea of a history of England under the Stuarts mooted by Ellis and himself in the late 1820s, although by 1831 he had become engaged on his abortive *History of France*.[69]

The tenor of these early essays on English history was one of striking emphasis on the spirit of the age, coupled with an overall radicalism much stronger than he would exhibit in the *History*. His Hampden essay, for all his wish to be courteous to the Whig Lord of the Treasury Lord Nugent, whose book on the subject he was then reviewing, opens by introducing Hampden as 'the renowned leader of the Long Parliament, the first of those great English commoners whose plain addition of Mister has, to our [i.e. 'my'] ears, a more majestic sound than the proudest of the feudal titles'. (It is a melancholy irony that though Macaulay saw through the press only one of his works, that on the younger Pitt, in the two years between his peerage and his death, all his writings thereafter were commonly identified by editors and commentators as by 'Lord Macaulay': it is another that the most distinguished 'Mister' of his century should have been that literary adversary described by him as 'the rising hope of ... stern unbending Tories', W.E.Gladstone, who, lacking a liberal heritage of his own before his conversion to Liberalism, compensated afterwards by coolly if surreptitiously appropriating many of Macaulay's arguments from history while officially reproving his ghost for his uses of it.)[70]

The central point here is that history was still a subordinate consideration for Macaulay. He wanted to inform Whig ideology by use of the past. He was writing in the heat of partisan warfare: thus the Hallam essay was written when the Catholic Emancipation struggle had reached a new phase of bitterness with the advent of Wellington's anti-Catholic government in place of the conciliatory administrations of Canning and Goderich, and its contemptuous attack on the want of religious sincerity of Cranmer and Elizabeth in their anti-Catholic legislation was intended to call into question the moral probity of all forms of governmental persecution of religion. He answered the usual catch-cries about Bloody Mary Tudor and her burnings of Protestants by granting her the 'wretched excuse' of sincerity, as he put it when he returned to these arguments in his essay on Burleigh (April 1832), and declaring as he did there that Elizabeth's persecution of Catholics was

even more odious than the persecution with which her sister had harassed the Protestants. We say more odious. For Mary had at least the plea of fanaticism. She did nothing for her religion which she was not prepared to suffer for it. She had held it firmly under persecution. She fully believed it to be essential to salvation. If she burned the bodies of her subjects, it was in order to rescue their souls.... But what can be said in defence of a ruler who is at once indifferent and intolerant?

In the Hallam essay he contrasted the English Reformation with the Scottish and European Reformations:

Elsewhere worldliness was the tool of zeal. Here zeal was the tool of worldliness. A King, whose character may be best described by saying that he was despotism itself personified, unprincipled ministers, a rapacious aristocracy, a servile Parliament, such were the instruments by which England was delivered from the yoke of Rome. The work which had been begun by Henry, the murderer of his wives, was continued by Somerset, the murderer of his brother, and completed by Elizabeth, the murderer of her guest.

Professor F.C.Montague, the editor of the *Essays* in 1903, sneered that when Macaulay framed this sentence 'he thought only of vexing the gentlemen who wrote for the *Quarterly Review*'. This is to confuse the academic objective of hatred with the artistic objective of love. Macaulay wanted first and foremost to convince Daniel O'Connell and his priest-supported Irish mass movement thundering at the doors of Parliament for Catholic Emancipation that an English writer, in the ideological quarterly journal of an English political party, was prepared to go to the historical root of religious controversy to show their cause would get an English championship founded on a manifest search for justice. He wanted to dissolve the enchantment of King, Church and Tory government which relied on ancient hatreds to perpetuate itself. 'Sprung from brutal passion, nurtured by selfish policy, the Reformation in England displayed little of what had, in other countries, distinguished it, unflinching and unsparing devotion, boldness of speech, and singleness of eye.' The resurgent Catholics might well feel, he could hope, that they needed no further rhetoric of alienation when their wrongs were hurled into the light of day by the son of the great Protestant Evangelical. His personal rage at the part of Herries's treachery to Goderich in the making of the Wellington government was reflected in his remarks on Strafford a little later in the Hallam essay:

> He was the first of the Rats, the first of those statesmen whose patriotism has been only the coquetry of political prostitution, and whose profligacy has taught governments to adopt the old maxim of the slave-market, that it is cheaper to buy than to breed, to import defenders from an Opposition than to rear them in a Ministry. He was the first Englishman to whom a peerage was a sacrament of infamy, a baptism into the communion of corruption.[71]

The Hallam essay leaped at the opportunity to show in historical terms that the cause of Catholic Emancipation was naturally the cause of the more radical Whigs. The former Whigs among the Tory anti-Emancipationists, and indeed those Tory descendants of Whig great houses such as his future friend Lord Mahon, argued that they and their anti-Catholic mob supporters were in the true tradition of the Whig Protestant Revolution of 1688: it was Macaulay and his pro-Emancipationist allies who represented a heresy. Macaulay's answer was to argue that government legislation against Catholics was the descendant of the same kind of Royal tyranny, whether represented by Tudor persecution of the Catholics or Stuart persecution of the Puritans. Hence in 1828 he made little of the common ground in modern Whig and Tory ideological inheritances to be found in the settlement of 1688, and much of their obvious divisions as shown in the Civil War. He eagerly invoked Milton (who would hardly have objected) on Satan to show Strafford as the fallen Archangel of Parliamentary Opposition.

The mordant attacks on Charles I in the Hallam essay, as in the 'Milton', accord well with the embodiment of resistance to Catholic claims as exhibited by George III and George IV, each of whom played a critical part in delaying Emancipation to the point where its concession robbed it of any likelihood of expediting Catholic (especially Irish Catholic) sense of partnership in British society. The attacks, which recurred in the Hampden essay in late 1831, were reinforced in vehemence by William IV's blatant attempts to escape from the clutches of the Whig Reform ministers headed by Earl Grey. Macaulay was directly comparing William to Charles in these months. Both now and later his main charge against Charles was faithlessness, of which both George IV and William IV gave ample evidence. George was a turncoat from the Foxite Whigs, William a restless intriguer even when in ostensible accord with their heirs. Behind both was the ugly presence of their brother Ernest, Duke of Cumberland, heir to the throne from 1830 should the little princess Victoria die: such a figure of High Tory bigotry invited the building up of a great ideological arsenal against Royal government. Macaulay had ample cause to fear in the Duke of Cumberland the architect of either reaction or revolution should he come to the throne, and he had no wish to see England face a ruler such as Charles X of France whose attempted return to autocracy overthrew the Bourbons in 1830. It is George IV and Ernest who we must bear in mind in reading such lines as the passage in the Hallam essay on Charles's attempted arrest of the five members of the House of Commons:

> a tyrant, whose whole life was a lie, who hated the Constitution the more because he had been compelled to feign respect for it, and to whom his own honour and the love of his people were as nothing, would select such a crisis for some appalling violation of law, for some stroke which might remove the chiefs of an Opposition, and intimidate the herd.

It specifically related to Charles I above all, however; and by indicting Charles Macaulay intended to strike at the root of reaction in England, which seemed so clearly to show itself in the monarchy.[72]

But Macaulay was not a 'Whig historian' of the kind who would later seek to find England's salvation in its fidelity to an ancient constitution. For all the criticisms later made of Macaulay as lacking a European perspective, he showed himself a remarkable European in a strong, but limited, degree. His essay on Machiavelli had given one indication of that; his essay on Hallam gave another. He argued that in the fifteenth century throughout western Europe 'there existed restraints on the royal authority, fundamental laws, and representative assemblies... the government of Castile seems to have been as free as that of our own country. That of Arragon was beyond all question more so.' The tendency of the seventeenth century was one of general absolutism reinforced by the accretion of wealth and the acquisition of standing armies by European rulers.

The Long Parliament by its resolute stand against Charles averted the fate of European constitutions. But it had to do so by a revolution.

> Those who conceive that the parliamentary leaders were desirous merely to maintain the old constitution, and those who represent them as conspiring to subvert it, are equally in error. The old constitution, as we have attempted to show, could not be maintained. The progress of time, the increase of wealth, the diffusion of knowledge, the great change in the European system of war, rendered it impossible that any of the monarchies of the middle ages should continue to exist on the old footing. If the privileges of the people were to remain absolutely stationary, they would relatively retrograde....
>
> It was now, therefore, absolutely necessary to violate the formal part of the constitution, in order to preserve its spirit.

Macaulay did not stand by all the enactments of the Long Parliament: he naturally disagreed with its anti-Catholicism (though stressing the dangers of Catholic absolutist influence in the Court) and with its execution of Archbishop Laud (although he was otherwise nasty enough about that unfortunate prelate). As to Laud, the violence and self-interest of nineteenth-century Protestant parsons against Catholic Emancipation had already found its outlet in Macaulay's satire 'The Country Clergyman's Trip to Cambridge': clerical zeal to subject the state to the divisive effects of defending Established Church power met a natural foe in the son of Zachary, however little Laudian theology actually resembled that of Macaulay's reverend targets. Macaulay repudiated the killing of King Charles and asserted that its achievement was made possible only by the destruction or injury of much of what republicans had wished to retain in the constitution. And he condemned it as folly: 'the blow which terminated his life at once transferred the allegiance of every Royalist to an heir, and an heir who was at liberty. To kill the individual was, under such circumstances, not to destroy, but to release the King.' The inference was that the monarchy deserved to exist only because it was so difficult to abolish. There followed a startling defence of Cromwell against Hallam's argument that he was inferior to Napoleon, a defence in which Macaulay did the pioneer shock-work for which Carlyle was later to take the credit. It praised Cromwell as a true representative of English middle-class sentiment, as a wise and forbearing statesman avoiding Napoleonic adventures abroad, and as a shrewd and effective international diplomat. It quite definitely regretted that Richard Cromwell's folly had destroyed his father's regime. Otherwise,

> We might now be writing under the government of his Highness Oliver the Fifth or Richard the Fourth, Protector, by the grace of God, of the Commonwealth of England, Scotland, and Ireland, and the dominions thereto belonging.[73]

His account of the reign of Charles II argued an utter collapse in public morality caused by the need for constant coat-turning by politicians in the violent vicissitudes of government and political ascendancies between 1640 and 1690. Breaking away from the restraints which Hallam's constitutional preoccupations had placed on him, he examined the manners and culture of the times as illustrations of their political bankruptcy. He chose a startling personal example, the future Duke of Marlborough:

> The history of Churchill shows, more clearly perhaps than that of any other individual, the malignity and extent of the corruption which had eaten into the heart of the public morality. An English gentleman of good family attaches himself to a Prince who has seduced his sister, and accepts rank and wealth as the price of her shame and his own. He then repays by ingratitude the benefits which he has purchased by ignominy, betrays his patron in a manner which the best cause cannot excuse, and commits an act, not only of private treachery, but of distinct military desertion. To his conduct at the crisis of the fate of James no service in modern times has, as far as we remember, furnished any parallel.... In our age and country, no talents, no services, no party attachments, could bear any man up under such mountains of infamy.

Macaulay saw politics under William III as equally destitute of public morality:

> It may well be conceived that, at such a time, such a nature as that of Marlborough would riot in the very luxury of baseness.

His former treason, thoroughly furnished with all that makes infamy exquisite, placed him under the disadvantage which attends every artist from the time that he produces a masterpiece. Yet his second great stroke may excite wonder, even in those who appreciate all the merit of the first. Lest his admirers should be able to say that at the time of the Revolution he had betrayed his King from any other than selfish motives, he proceeded to betray his country. He sent intelligence to the French court of a secret expedition intended to attack Brest. The consequence was that the expedition failed, and that eight hundred British soldiers lost their lives from the abandoned villainy of a British general. Yet this man has been canonized by so many eminent writers that to speak of him as he deserves may seem scarcely decent.

The view thus expressed of Marlborough was to be amplified in the *History*. Why was so much made of it here? Macaulay had taken his charges from a source equally hostile to Marlborough, Hallam's book, itself built at this point on the revelations from the Jacobite documents printed by Dalrymple. When the *History* appeared, Macaulay was somewhat unreasonably singled out for abuse by defenders of Marlborough merely for reasserting what earlier authorities had printed. But he attracted their spleen by the colour of his writing, so memorable in comparison to Hallam's deliberately cold prose. Once again, the cause of making an example of Marlborough in the Hallam essay would seem to have been at hand in the politics of the time of writing: Macaulay had seen his hopes of Catholic Emancipation and its peaceful resolution placed at hazard by the sudden formation of an extreme Tory government under another military hero in politics. He certainly never entertained an estimate of Wellington embracing the slightest suspicion of treachery, personal or national (though at this time he took him to be very lukewarm against slavery and told Zachary that the Duke's speech of 23 June 1828 was 'as bad as possible'). He wanted to warn against the cult of the military hero as political idol, implying that personal glory would be adverse to the interests of a constitutional state. Once the constitution had broken down a military hero might be acceptable, provided he could govern with the success of a Cromwell. But domestic politics brought out the worst in creatures of such talents and ambition. And Wellington's

name was coupled with that of Marlborough above all other Englishmen: to highlight the infamy of Marlborough might rob Wellington of some of the dubious political effects of his fame. He also
was attracted by the artistic possibilities of such portraiture, as the
passage makes clear: Dante and Milton were challenges and exemplars to him. Some years later he would thrust a Dantean view of
the politics of the period into the commencement of his essay on Sir
William Temple (*Edinburgh*, October 1838), in which Marlborough
is left in the final and utmost hell, 'the eternal ice of Giudecca'.
Halifax by that time had travelled high in his estimation from the
contemptuous dismissal he was given in the Hallam essay; but however bardic a flourish Giudecca might have been, there Marlborough
would always remain.[74]

As for the Revolution of 1688 itself, the essay on Hallam could
hardly have been more hostile to its makers:

> The great improvement which took place in our breed of public
> men is principally to be ascribed to the Revolution. Yet that
> memorable event, in a great measure, took its character from
> the very vices which it was the means of reforming. It was assur-
> edly a happy revolution, and a useful revolution; but it was not,
> what it has often been called, a glorious revolution. William,
> and William alone, derived glory from it. The transaction was,
> in almost every part, discreditable to England. That a tyrant who
> had violated the fundamental laws of the country, who had
> attacked the rights of its greatest corporations, who had begun
> to persecute the established religion of the state, who had never
> respected the law either in his superstition or in his revenge,
> could not be pulled down without the aid of a foreign army,
> is a circumstance not very grateful to our national pride. Yet
> this is the least degrading part of the story. The shameless insin-
> cerity of the great and noble, the warm assurances of general
> support which James received, down to the moment of general
> desertion, indicate a meanness of spirit and a looseness of mora-
> lity most disgraceful to the age. That the enterprise succeeded,
> at least that it succeeded without bloodshed or commotion, was
> principally owing to an act of ungrateful perfidy, such as no
> soldier had ever before committed, and to those monstrous fic-
> tions respecting the birth of the Prince of Wales which persons
> of the highest rank were not ashamed to circulate. In all the

proceedings of the convention, in the conference particularly, we see that littleness of mind which is the chief characteristic of the times. The resolutions on which the two Houses at last agreed were as bad as any resolutions for so excellent a purpose could be. Their feeble and contradictory language was evidently intended to save the credit of the Tories, who were ashamed to name what they were not ashamed to do. Through the whole transaction no commanding talents were displayed by any Englishman; no extraordinary risks were run; no sacrifices were made for the deliverance of the nation except the sacrifice which Churchill made of honour, and Anne of natural affection.

As Professor John Kenyon observes in *The History Men*, everything here is contained in the *History* 'or can easily be deduced from it, yet the tone is radically different, and so is the viewpoint'. But the contour remains the same: so we are faced with the irony that Macaulay's *History* was first conceived within an essay largely attuned to, and prompted by, the immediate political crises of its time of writing, and thereby a tension of a most constructive kind was created in the *History* itself. As Chesterton said, there are two Macaulays, but he was not wholly accurate in seeing the Romantic Macaulay as earlier and the Whig Macaulay as later. The *History* would deviate from the Hallam essay at certain points with more rather than less Romanticism. The Whig interpretation of history might seem to have more in common with the Hallam essay, and its assumption of the inexorable working out of progress independent of the moral character exhibited by the makers of that progress. It was less in tune with a narrative whose greatest affection is given to the ironic, anti-popular, cultured Halifax who preferred to incline to the losing side, who was so slow to embrace the Revolution, and whose public services were terminated by the factiousness of the Whigs. And if Macaulay changed in his estimate of the Revolution he retained his admiration for the Long Parliament, all the more as his view of it was unsullied by any depth of primary research. At the close of the first part of the *History* his paean in praise of the Revolution of 1688 for having averted in Britain the horrors which came to pass in 1848 has the unexpected inclusion of the Long Parliament among the other obvious candidates for gratitude – God, the Convention (now redeemed in his eyes) and William of Orange.[75]

Although the immediate aftermath of the huge essay on Hallam was Macaulay's idea of a history of England under the Stuarts, intended to have the rich social and cultural texture so conspicuously lacking in Hallam's austerely constitutional treatise, he did not return to the history of the Revolution of 1688 until seven years had passed. The Hampden essay was followed by a slight essay on Mirabeau and the dawn of the French Revolution (*Edinburgh*, July 1832), and this by a lively discussion of Lord Mahon's account of the War of the Succession in Spain during Anne's reign (January 1833). This latter essay was distinguished by its defence of the Tory-made Peace of Utrecht, a little on the lines on which he had previously discussed the Revolution, denouncing the men and applauding the measure. He pointedly differed from his Tory friend's support of his Whig ancestors' opposition to Utrecht, applying common-sense argument on the merits of the peace for its own sake: the continuation of the war could gain no further lasting advantage for Britain's policies and must result in even further ghastly carnage. Mahon had given him an excellent reminder that the supposedly Whig Revolution continued to bring aid and comfort to modern Tories, and that its defence buttressed their arguments. As a modern Whig Macaulay was no friend to European coalitions intent on forcing foreign-made settlements on countries against their own wishes. The Spain of his own time beaten down under the Congress system gave him lessons for the Spain of Anne's.

Yet he was being subtly drawn more and more into history for its own sake as the urgencies of political life receded with the achievement of Reform. The character of the essays began to change from commentaries on history to historical narrative and analysis for its own sake. He produced two remarkable essays on eighteenth-century English history (October 1833 and January 1834): one, initially an analysis of Horace Walpole as man of letters, becoming a remarkably sympathetic discussion of Sir Robert Walpole's long rule as Premier, his search for peace and his supersession by increasingly less competent critics; the other a cool, ironic exploration of the early life of the elder Pitt, mocking in its presentation of his inconsistency and dramatic posturing, but admiring of his great war leadership. These works were shot through with the use of literary sources, and with striking flourishes of social data. They were so far from the purely partisan that the two heroes were in fact bitter opponents, and a subordinate cameo could not fail to inspire affection in the reader for a statesman obnoxious to them both – Carteret. Above all they reflected Macaulay's love of Parliamentary battles transmitted with the excitement of a participant in the Reform struggles of 1830–32. He wrote from a sense of possession of the institution. He was also putting to good effect what he had heard of the Commons in the late eighteenth century from Lord Holland's recollections of Charles James Fox's stories, and from Wilberforce, who was first elected in 1780. His sources for speeches were at best often threadbare, and the very nature of his oral evidence and the old stories handed down by veterans which it produced, meant that he celebrated Parliament in those exotic moments which particularly excited folk memory. The essays stirred public attention partly because he served up so well that which had enabled his material to survive with whatever fidelity : he was becoming the historian for Everyman because of his dependence on the kind of evidence which Everyman relished. His having a good working knowledge of the Commons before Reform meant that he could discuss manoeuvres with the concentration of a neo-phyte observer of political crisis, and assess debate with the skills of a chess champion reviewing past Grandmasters. Inevitably his artistic success in making the most of such sparse materials led him to assign greater value to his deductions than was wise, and (for all his frequent warnings on the dearth of satisfactory reports) to assume his own control of the Parliamentary past more than was justified. Specifically, his own status as a Capablanca of debate meant that he could enthral his audience with a sense of debate's capacity to stir the blood as thoroughly as any battle narrative, but it also meant that he created a sense of the significance of Parliament for his immediate audience and for posterity which came to see the effects of Parliamentary debate and manoeuvre out of proportion. Parliament mattered to him, therefore it must matter to everyone. And it mattered far more to him than it had done in the days of the essay on Hallam when he was an outsider to its activities, however much he made of the debates he witnessed before his election in 1830.

The affection exhibited when he wrote about Parliamentary history was from the first startlingly at variance with the attitude of many makers of revolution. He and his colleagues had brought an old system to its end in 1832, or so he believed, but he was hostile from the first to any dismissal of the unreformed Commons as lacking the basis for respect which the more representative system invited. He would be attacked for writing history with an eye to the present, and we have seen this was how he came to write it, but as his devotion to history grew he showed himself an envenomed opponent of judgment of the past by present-day standards. Reviewing the posthumous publication of Sir James Mackintosh's unfinished *History of the Revolution in England, in 1688* (*Edinburgh*, July 1835) he made a ferocious attack on its anonymous but egregious editor:

> Nothing in the Memoir or in the Continuation of the history has struck us so much as the contempt with which the writer thinks fit to speak of all things that were done before the coming in of the very last fashions in politics. We think that we have sometimes observed a leaning towards the same fault in persons of a much higher order of intellect....
>
> ... the very considerations which lead us to look forward with sanguine hope to the future prevent us from looking back with contempt on the past. We do not flatter ourselves with the notion that we have attained perfection, and that no more truth remains to be found. We believe that we are wiser than our ancestors. We believe, also, that our posterity will be wiser than we. It would be gross injustice in our grandchildren to talk of us with contempt, merely because they may have surpassed us.... As we would have our descendants judge us, so ought we to judge our fathers. In order to form a correct estimate of their merits, we ought to place ourselves in their situation, to put out of our minds, for a time, all that knowledge which they, however eager in the pursuit of truth, could not have, and which we, however negligent we may have been, could not help having. It was not merely difficult, but absolutely impossible, for the best and greatest of men, two hundred years ago, to be what a very commonplace person in our days may easily be, and indeed must necessarily be. But it is too much that the benefactors of mankind, after having been reviled by the dunces of their own generation for going too far, should be reviled by the dunces of the next generation for not going far enough.

The argument assumed that 'the science of government is an experimental science, and that, like all other experimental sciences, it is generally in a state of progression'. Mackintosh's own training in the Edinburgh medical school, the foremost of its day, may have inspired Macaulay to couch his argument strongly in analogy to medical progress:

> Sydenham first discovered that the cool regimen succeeded best in cases of small-pox. By this discovery he saved the lives of hundreds of thousands; and we venerate his memory for it, though he never heard of inoculation. Lady Mary Wortley Montague brought inoculation into use; and we respect her for it, though she never heard of vaccination. Jenner introduced vaccination; we admire him for it, and we shall continue to admire him for it, although some still safer and more agreeable preservative should be discovered.

There are obvious arguments in rejection of this thesis; but to recite them is to tumble into the trap he so charmingly prepared for us, his 'grandchildren'. Few of his critics have avoided it, and with all their indictments, there he is, laughing at us.[76]

Macaulay's Parliamentarianism owed something to his long campaign to reclaim Burke for the cause of liberty. He was deeply drawn to Burke's veneration for history, and to his profound analysis of men and events in the past. But it went two ways. In the Hallam essay he stated grimly near the conclusion:

> The conflict of the seventeenth century was maintained by the Parliament against the Crown. The conflict which commenced in the middle of the eighteenth century, which still [i.e. in 1828] remains undecided, and in which our children and grandchildren will probably be called to act or to suffer, is between a large portion of the people on the one side, and the Crown and the Parliament united on the other.

By the time of the Hampden essay he was in Parliament, although far from certain that the Reform struggle would be resolved without violence, but his championship of Hampden was the championship of a hero he took to be a great Parliamentarian, although one ultimately driven to take up arms in defence of Parliament's cause. In his peroration lay a regret that the great Parliamentarian should have been killed in 1643, and that with him perished the possibility of moderation, by implication born of his mastery of the arts of peace. Inevitably this diminished Cromwell, who owed his rise to the arts of war. The peroration was bardic exaggeration, but behind its veneration of Hampden was the hope that Parliament would yet reform itself peacefully and that the moderate leadership of Grey would bring a resolution without violence, as indeed happened:

> in Hampden, and in Hampden alone, were united all the qualities which, at such a crisis, were necessary to save the state.... Others might possess the qualities which were necessary to save the popular party in the crisis of danger; he alone had both the power and the inclination to restrain its excesses in the hour of triumph. Others could conquer; he alone could reconcile... it was when to the sullen tyranny of Laud and Charles had succeeded the fierce conflict of sects and factions, ambitious of ascendancy and burning for revenge, it was when the vices and ignorance which the old tyranny had generated threatened the new freedom with destruction, that England missed the sobriety, the self-command, the perfect soundness of judgment, the perfect rectitude of intention, to which the history of revolutions furnishes no parallel, or furnishes a parallel in Washington alone.

It was this which enabled Thomas Carlyle in the sixth (22 May 1840) of his lectures on *Heroes, Hero-Worship and the Heroic in History* to ignore the Hallam essay's tribute to Cromwell (with which, as a fellow contributor to the *Edinburgh*, he would have been acquainted), and to complain:

> One Puritan, I think, and almost he alone, our poor Cromwell, seems to hang yet on the gibbet, and find no hearty apologist anywhere. Him neither saint nor sinner will acquit of great wickedness. A man of ability, infinite talent, courage, and so forth: but he betrayed the Cause.... And then there come contrasts with Washington and others; above all, with these noble Pyms and Hampdens, whose noble work he stole for himself, and ruined into a futility and deformity....
>
> For my own share, far be it from me to say or insinuate a word of disparagement against such characters as Hampden, Eliot, Pym; whom I believe to have been right worthy and useful men. I have read diligently what books and documents about

them I could come at; — with the honestest wish to admire, to
live and worship them like Heroes; but I am sorry to say, if
the real truth must be told, with very indifferent success! At
bottom, I found that it would not do. They are very noble men
these; step along in their stately way, with their measured
euphuisms, philosophies, parliamentary eloquences, Ship-
moneys, *Monarchies of Man*; a most constitutional, unblamable,
dignified set of men. But the heart remains cold to them; the
fancy alone endeavours to get-up some worship of them. What
man's heart does, in reality, break-forth into any fire of brotherly
love for these men? They are become dreadfully dull men!

Carlyle's self-serving omissions should not cloud the issue. It is idle
to say that Macaulay paid eloquent tribute to Cromwell even as
he idolized Hampden, and that Carlyle's denial of fire breaking
forth in any 'man's heart' for Hampden is a deliberate attempt to
pretend away Macaulay's success in finding poetry in Parliament.
He nonetheless set his finger on the great difference between himself
and Macaulay, as Macaulay had now become. Macaulay henceforth
saw Parliament as the means by which Britain would progress where
she could and preserve what she should; Carlyle saw it as a stupid
and irrelevant mystification. Cromwell henceforth remained a hero
to them both, but to Macaulay he was the pattern of benevolent
despotism when preferable means of government had broken down,
whereas to Carlyle he was inspiration without qualification. It was
the struggle of Parliamentarian against anti-Parliamentarian, and
Carlyle never forgave Macaulay for investing what he regarded as
a dull institution for small men with fire, excitement and romance.
Hence he termed Macaulay a fictionist of an 'essentially irremedi-
able, commonplace nature'. Macaulay was as uncomplimentary,
and in his turn sought to side-step the danger of Carlyle by dismissing
him as absurd. But the sharpening of Macaulay's admiration for
Parliament may have owed much to his awareness of the attractiveness of Carlyle's cult of the ruthless, unfettered hero. The hidden
debate between them became more explicit after Macaulay's death,
when many of his foremost critics, and ultimately his nephew-
biographer, confronted his life and writings in the intoxication of
the Carlylean. That debate divided Hitler's Europe from its Western
opponents in World War II. For all of the complaint that Macaulay
from the mid-1830s appeared to invite complacency, posterity owes

him much for his efforts to enchant it with his enthusiasm for representative government. If those who imitate his adulation for it lack his constructive originality, it is not his fault.[77]

Carlyle in that lecture on 'The Hero as King' declared 'this of Puritanism had got itself hushed-up into decent composure, and its results made smooth, in 1688'; it was that process which had won the abiding gratitude of Burke (Irish effects excepted), which absorbed the uncompleted labours of Mackintosh, and to which Macaulay would later devote the great task of his life. Even as he was swinging to Parliamentarianism in the Hampden essay he continued to find the respectable Revolution a subject for unfavourable contrast with his still much-abused Parliamentarian hero. It turned on a particularly ironic point for his own half-repressed Scottish identity: were Hampden and his friends guilty of treason in inviting the Scots in arms against Charles to invade England, then a different kingdom under the same King?

It is said that to call in the aid of foreigners in a domestic quarrel is the worst of treasons, and that the Puritan leaders, by taking this course, showed that they were regardless of the honour and independence of the nation, and anxious only for the success of their own faction. We are utterly unable to see any distinction between the case of the Scotch invasion in 1640, and the case of the Dutch invasion in 1688; or rather, we see distinctions which are to the advantage of Hampden and his friends. We believe Charles to have been a worse and more dangerous king than his son. The Dutch were strangers to us, the Scots a kindred people speaking the same language, subjects of the same prince, not aliens in the eye of the law. If, indeed, it had been possible that a Scotch army or a Dutch army could have enslaved England, those who persuaded Leslie to cross the Tweed, and those who signed the invitation to the Prince of Orange, would have been traitors to their country. But such a result was out of the question. All that either a Scotch or a Dutch invasion could do was to give the public feeling of England an opportunity to show itself. Both expeditions would have ended in complete and ludicrous discomfiture, had Charles and James been supported by their soldiers and their people.

So even then the affair of 1688 looked more dubious than the Puritan

Revolution. It might seem that Macaulay's view in 1831 was still close to Carlyle's testy summation delivered nine years later (prompting the thought – horror of horrors! – that Carlyle had been influenced by his reading of the young Macaulay). But the Mackintosh essay in 1835 is the first firmly to applaud the makers of the Revolution of 1688 for themselves rather than simply as unworthy agents of the logical working-out of processes of progress inaugurated by far better men. In part this was defensiveness towards his own Reform Act: it had not, after all, inaugurated the millennium, however apocalyptic the struggle had seemed. Macaulay, especially chafing against Mackintosh's editor (who denounced the harsh anti-Catholic limits of liberty accorded in the 1688 Settlement), began to think more kindly of legislators in former times unsure of their room for manoeuvre.

> The principle on which the authors of the Revolution acted cannot be mistaken. They were perfectly aware that the English institutions stood in need of reform. But they also knew that an important point was gained if they could settle once for all, by a solemn compact, the matters which had, during several generations, been in controversy between the Parliament and the Crown. They therefore most judiciously abstained from mixing up the irritating and perplexing question of what ought to be the law with the plain question of what was the law.... Whigs and Tories were generally agreed as to the illegality of the dispensing power and of taxation imposed by the royal prerogative... if the Parliament had determined to revise the whole constitution, and to provide new securities against misgovernment, before proclaiming the new sovereign, months would have been lost in disputes. The coalition which had delivered the country would have been instantly dissolved.... If the the authors of the Revolution had been fools enough to take this course, we have little doubt that Luxembourg would have been upon them in the midst of their constitution-making. They might have been interrupted in a debate on Filmer's and Sydney's theories of government by the entrance of the musketeers of Louis's household, and have been marched off, two and two, to frame imaginary monarchies and commonwealths in the Tower.

And he cited the cases of the contemporary revolutions in Spain and Naples which he saw as having been overthrown because 'the friends of liberty wasted in discussions upon abstract questions the time which ought to have been employed in preparing for national defence':

> Thank God, our deliverers were men of a very different order from the Spanish and Neapolitan legislators. They might, on many subjects, hold opinions which, in the nineteenth century, would not be considered as liberal. But they were not dreaming pedants. They were statesmen accustomed to the management of great affairs.

In twentieth-century terms, it was the question which divided the Spanish Republic in 1936–37, whether to work within a coalition to defend the Republic against Franco and his allies, Hitler and Mussolini, or to fight the war while simultaneously using its revolutionary sentiment to produce internal social revolution. The Stalinists upheld the former position, the anarcho-syndicalists the latter. Macaulay, always the firm admirer of William of Orange, used the arguments later to be taken up by the Stalinists: at least he had the excuse that his Stalin risked his neck in the conflict. His position was certainly far less unhistorical than that of the (Irish Catholic) editor he was criticizing: a more radical revolution would have been more anti-Catholic, not less. The English mob was at its most incendiary in hatred of Catholicism, as Macaulay well knew from his own lifetime. This is, in fact, one of the most powerful origins of his own hatred of mob rule. His *History* might argue in 1848 that it was the moderation of the 1688 Settlement and its endurance which acted as a prophylactic against future revolution; he might have added, though he did not, that its own long-term revolutionary effects in institutionalizing anti-Catholicism laid London in ruins in 1780 on the cry of 'No Popery!'[78]

To Professor Kenyon what had happened was that 'from 1832 or thereabouts [Macaulay] turned to the Whiggism of the grandees, of Holland House, Devonshire House, Woburn and Chatsworth, the Whiggism of broad acres and a balanced constitution, to whom 1688, and only 1688, was the Year 1 of Liberty'. Macaulay breeds unconscious imitators in bardic hyperbole! He had in reality little connection with these places, apart from Holland House where his career as an acolyte was intense but short. He got a kick out of it at the time, as well as a few fan-smacks, and it was in part a kick in the direction Professor Kenyon indicates, but his exuberance in being part of such circles greatly declined when he had no Margaret to tell of them and Hannah was preoccupied with Trevelyan. Subsequently his involvement with great houses was chiefly with an eye to their archives. Certainly his material would have given him an aristocratic preoccupation, but this is more the occupational disease of a historian than of a socialite. Even at Holland House it was the oral evidence giving him purchase on the past which seems most to have pleased him, and here Mackintosh's friendship was important. The Mackintosh essay was chiefly animated by anger at his old friend's work having been put out with a continuation and a memoir which seemed to detract from the spirit and achievements of its author. He got it off from India just before he heard of Margaret's death. Mackintosh's heirs were evidently seriously disturbed by his anger (though the real culprits were the profit-hungry publishers, Longmans), the work was reissued later in 1835 without the alien material, and on Macaulay's return he was given Mackintosh's superb collection on the Revolution. (He also acquired a chastened publisher for the future.) The essay in its loyalty to Mackintosh made absurd claims for the excellence of what was but a patchy and ill-organized fragment, noble, humane, judicious and possessed of many insights but far from being a major historical work. It practically implied that Mackintosh swept the field.

The great break in waiting for the *Edinburgh* followed, and Macaulay's next enterprise, on Bacon, suggests that so far as he could have any major literary plans they still concerned a survey of the entire seventeenth century. Writing to Ellis from India on 30 December 1835 he spoke of his desire to quit politics and

to undertake some great historical work which may be at once the business and the amusement of my life... that a man before whom the two paths of literature and politics lie open, and who might hope for eminence in either, should chuse politics and quit literature seems to me madness.... Who would compare the fame of Charles Townshend to that of Hume, that of Lord North to that of Gibbon, that of Lord Chatham to that of Johnson? – Who can look back on the Life of Burke, and not regret that the years which he passed in ruining his health and temper by political exertions were not passed in the composition of some great and durable work?

A year and a day later he was expressing a similar wish to quit politics, this time to his friend Mahon, in thanking him for the first volume of his (ultimately seven-volume) *History of England* which was to span the eighteenth century from 1713 to 1783: 'it is the best history of George the First's reign'. Thus the design that he ultimately formed must trespass on ground where two friends had already won his high praise. But the huge, invaluable and largely unused Mackintosh collection would have been the determining factor in deciding Macaulay to begin his great book with the Revolution, and Mackintosh's fragment was forgotten because of Macaulay's own archival diligence.[79]

One other consideration which brought Macaulay back to later seventeenth-century England was the pull of its literature. His interest in Swift and in the literary controversies of the past led him naturally to try an essay on Sir William Temple's life and works; but when he got Courtenay's edition of them for review he was overjoyed by its materials for social history as well as excited by its revelations of diplomatic history, and the resultant essay (*Edinburgh*, October 1838) made for an elegant study of a man who saw the troubled times of the late seventeenth century from the safest place he could find. The Bacon essay (*Edinburgh*, June 1837) is by contrast overshadowed with gloom: the author admires Bacon's mind, is all the quicker to condemn Bacon for ingratitude, servility, cruelty and corruption, reaches his verdict with the hard, intolerant heat of India, and is in any case still in the first agony of his private wound. The Temple essay is the work of a man who loved his England and was very glad to be home. All the more does it dart about, taking repossession of a history which means English love-letters, and English theories of government, and English countryside, and English scholarly controversies, and English journeys to the Continent: Macaulay seems to have recovered some of the delight of a child returning to its beloved home after boarding school, finding far more fascination in the old favourite spots, and exploring new nooks and crannies hardly examined before. The essay thus becomes an overture to the *History* (which formally he began a few months after the essay's appearance in October 1838), and the delicacy and sympathy of its portrait of Dorothy Osborne give it a human quality quite of its own.

The remaining essays include other overtures. That on Gladstone's theories of Church and state is officially non-historical, but
handles questions of the state's duties to serve the specific Established Church and the consequent abridgment of the liberties of
other religious sects with great force: Macaulay would always see
the seventeenth-century struggle as depending on this precise point.
His greatest, and growing, objection to James II would be that he
sought to repossess the Church of England for Roman Catholicism
at the ultimate expense of religious liberty: but if after 1688 the
Church of England remained safely Protestant and the Church of
Scotland safely Presbyterian, he was just as embattled against their
self-aggrandizement at the expense of other British subjects. To the
end of his life he blamed James for making Roman Catholicism
a symbol of state oppression in England, and hence making its emancipation so long, hazardous and painful an experience. The Gladstone essay was finished two days before the *History* was
commenced, on 7 and 9 March 1839 respectively. The Ranke essay,
written in September 1840, was partly to discuss the whole history
of Roman Catholicism and to examine the dynamics of the Counter-
Reformation whose effects must be indicated in his *History* – the
origin of the Jesuits, and why they would support a bold policy
of Roman Catholic repossession of English institutions from James,
and the considerations of papal politics, which would lead Popes
Innocent XI and Alexander VIII in their hostility to Louis XIV to
seek to restrain James and lend covert support to William. Yet to
inform his readers and himself he stepped into the broadest chronological sweep he ever attempted, and caught the enthusiasm of
Roman Catholicism in its popular as well as in its official expression.
It was appropriate in that the vicissitudes of its history in England
had determined the course of Macaulay's political beginnings and,
as it would happen, his effective political end. The most famous
passage in the essay was to be used by his enemies in the making
of that end:

> There is not, and there never was on this earth, a work of human
> policy so well deserving of examination as the Roman Catholic
> Church. The history of that Church joins together the two great
> ages of human civilization. No other institution is left standing
> which carries the mind back to the times when the smoke of

sacrifice rose from the Pantheon, and when camelopards and tigers bounded in the Flavian amphitheatre. The proudest royal houses are but of yesterday, when compared with the line of Supreme Pontiffs. . . . The Papacy remains, not in decay, not a mere antique, but full of life and youthful vigour. The Catholic Church is still sending forth to the farthest ends of the world, missionaries as zealous as those who landed in Kent with Augustin, and still confronting hostile kings with the same spirit with which she confronted Attila. The number of her children is greater than in any former age. . . . Nor do we see any sign which indicates that the term of her long dominion is approaching. She saw the commencement of all the governments and of all the ecclesiastical establishments that now exist in the world; and we feel no assurance that she is not destined to see the end of them all. She was great and respected before the Saxon had set foot on Britain, before the Frank had passed the Rhine, when Grecian eloquence still flourished in Antioch, when idols were still worshipped in the temple of Mecca. And she may still exist in undiminished vigour when some traveller from New Zealand shall, in the midst of a vast solitude, take his stand on a broken arch of London Bridge to sketch the ruins of St Paul's.

If the sentences gave a Roman Catholic a greater sense of participation in his United Kingdom to hear such language from so conspicuous an English nationalist, that alone would have been an adequate recompense.[80]

The essay on Leigh Hunt's edition of Restoration Comedies (January 1841) was his last foray in essay form into the field of his *History*, and it was a ferocious reassertion of his contempt for the morality of the age as exhibited by the licentiousness of its drama. Macaulay speaks with disdain of any notion of censorship, adding in his best bardic hyperbolics:

The Athenian Comedies, in which there are scarcely a hundred lines together without some passage of which Rochester would have been ashamed, have been reprinted at the Pitt Press, and the Clarendon Press, under the direction of syndics and delegates appointed by the Universities, and have been illustrated with notes by reverend, very reverend, and right reverend commentators. Every year the most distinguished young men in the kingdom

are examined by bishops and professors of divinity in such works
as the Lysistrata of Aristophanes and the Sixth Satire of Juvenal.
There is certainly something a little ludicrous in the idea of a
conclave of venerable fathers of the church praising and reward-
ing a lad on account of his intimate acquaintance with writings
compared with which the loosest tale in Prior is modest. But,
for our own part, we have no doubt that the greatest societies
which direct the education of the English gentry have herein
judged wisely.

He was firm that classical learning improved the statesman and
the churchman, while

we find it difficult to believe that, in a world so full of temptation
as this, any gentleman whose life would have been virtuous if
he had not read Aristophanes and Juvenal will be made vicious
by reading them. A man who, exposed to all the influences of
such a state of society as that in which we live, is yet afraid
of exposing himself to the influences of a few Greek or Latin
verses, acts, we think, much like the felon who begged the sheriffs
to let him have an umbrella held over his head from the door
of Newgate to the gallows, because it was a drizzling morning,
and he was apt to take cold.

What disgusted him about the plays of the forty years after the
Restoration was their sexism: 'the whole body of the dramatists
invariably represent adultery, we do not say as a peccadillo, we
do not say as an error which the violence of passion may excuse,
but as the calling of a fine gentleman, as a grace without which
his character would be imperfect.' He saw it as a disastrous change
from the ethics of drama in the time of Elizabeth and James I,
put it down to the repression of manners during the Commonwealth
when theatres were closed and a sanctimonious appearance was
taken as the best proof of God's favour, and insisted that censorship
induced hypocrisy followed by public profligacy at its worst. He
added that Leigh Hunt had performed a service by putting such
valuable sources for social history before the public 'though we
certainly cannot recommend the handsome volume before us as
an appropriate Christmas present for young ladies'. His love for
his sisters gave him a fine insight into the peculiarly nauseating

forms of male chauvinism masquerading as liberty of artistic expression; he understood the stifling destruction in women's relegation to sex objects whose acquisition was deemed proof of masculinity. And his account of Jeremy Collier, naturally obnoxious to him as a High Church Jacobite, becomes, as Chesterton says, 'almost Homeric' in his account of Collier's attack on the pestiferous fashion of contemporary drama:

> It is inspiriting to see how gallantly the solitary outlaw advances to attack enemies, formidable separately, and, it might have been thought, irresistible when combined, distributes his swashing blows right and left among Wycherley, Congreve, and Vanbrugh, treads the wretched D'Urfey down in the dirt beneath his feet, and strikes with all his strength full at the towering crest of Dryden.

After all, Macaulay was not prepared to allow his earlier indictment of the morality of 1688 to be swept aside merely because he had acquired a higher respect for the pragmatism of the Convention Parliament.[81]

The essays of the 1840s, and indeed the biographies for the *Encyclopaedia Britannica* in the 1850s, are works of sufficient maturity to be adjudged histories in miniature. For a time Macaulay's cherished hopes of encompassing the eighteenth century within his *History* made him a little unhappy about using material he might later wish to incorporate in it – on 1 December 1841 he wrote to Napier that 'I a little grudge you' the account of the trial of Warren Hastings on those grounds: apparently he did not imagine that the Indian matter in the essays on Clive and Hastings would much occupy him in the *History*. Of these essays themselves perhaps the major point to underline was Macaulay's iron insistence on political probity and honourable dealing among imperial representatives: he held partisan judicial conduct in especial horror. In his scheme of an England in which all creeds and races were to participate, dissolving as much as possible of their alien cultures, the insistence on equality under the law was vital. In 'Hallam' he singled out the Bench and Bar of Charles II's reign as 'the spots and blemishes of our legal chronicles'. In the *History* he reached an obvious height of personal horror in recounting the sadism and bias of Judge Jeffreys, especially in his 'Bloody Assize' trying suspects of complicity in the Monmouth

Revolt. (Macaulay's humanitarian fury led him into some distortion of the record here, though in reproving him his critics with less excuse have also distorted it.) He wrote with loathing of his hero Robert Clive's use of perjury and forgery to free himself of the dangers posed by the potential treachery of an influential and untrustworthy Indian:

> That honesty is the best policy is a maxim which we firmly believe to be generally correct, even with respect to the temporal interests of individuals; but, with respect to societies, the rule is subject to still fewer exceptions, and that, for this reason, that the life of societies is longer than the life of individuals. It is possible to mention men who have owed great worldly prosperity to breaches of private faith. But we doubt whether it is possible to mention a state which has on the whole been a gainer by a breach of public faith. The entire history of British India is an illustration of the great truth, that it is not prudent to oppose perfidy by perfidy, and that the most efficient weapon with which men can encounter falsehood is truth.

This may be incorrect – he would shortly be writing his essay on Frederick the Great, who seemed to prove it incorrect for himself and his country, and whose great breach of faith against Maria Theresa in Macaulay's view caused untold suffering to others rather than himself:

> On the head of Frederic is all the blood which was shed in a war which raged during many years and in every quarter of the globe, the blood of the column of Fontenoy, the blood of the mountaineers who were slaughtered at Culloden. The evils produced by his wickedness were felt in lands where the name of Prussia was unknown; and, in order that he might rob a neighbour whom he had promised to defend, black men fought on the coast of Coromandel, and red men scalped each other by the Great Lakes of North America.

It was his bardic self run riot; and it is the bard in mourning. Among other things – including his ancestors' fellow Highlanders – it mourns the inapplicability of his general maxim as coined in the context of Clive. But however wrong he may have been in that, the world was the better for a man who wrote in such terms for so wide an audience. His master Edmund Burke would have approved his resolute opposition to Machiavellian ethics. The same standard was evident in the Hastings essay, where indeed his use of Indian memories of Chief Justice Elijah Impey led him far beyond his evidence in order to excoriate what seemed to him the terrible spectacle of an unjust judge disgracing British law before new subjects who should have been induced to revere it.[82]

It may be argued from this that the essays on Clive and Hastings, although undertaken with the admirable enterprise of dissolving the public ignorance of the great country where Macaulay had laboured with such diligence and pain, were more tracts for the training of future British administrators and Indian students alike than history presented in its own terms. It is also true that they depended considerably on oral evidence with its inevitable exaggeration in an imperial context: he undoubtedly swelled the horror story of the Black Hole of Calcutta far beyond its original character. If these essays are only the reflections of a highly conscientious and thoughtful administrator on the origins of the power which he and his colleagues wielded, they merit consideration. Their problem was that, like so much else that he wrote, their prose was so vivid and so compelling that they were seriously regarded as standard history. In fact, they were essays, in the earlier sense in which he had written, with historical data as the instructive matter for his guides to posterity and explanation to his homeland. Their place for the historian is a different one to much of Macaulay's other work: they are major documents in the attempts of one part of the world to talk about another. Nevertheless the historian who sets aside Macaulay's assumptions because of their obvious biases and inadequacy of evidence would be mistaken, here as elsewhere. He raised important questions, he propounded important speculations, even if he frequently answered both in unjustifiable affirmatives.

I have been most concerned with the historical work of Macaulay's essays for the light they throw on his development as the future author of the *History*; but perhaps their most important service is that they inspire constructive reflections, and that the theories they put forward are not to be set aside merely because they are sometimes disguised as facts. His essays were essays: sometimes, as with the three on the elder and younger Pitt, they reach a level which cannot fail to bring history to life before the reader and bring much wheat as well as cockle in their harvest. Sometimes they are interesting chiefly as the thoughts of a very lively and vastly stocked mind, over-conscious of what it had witnessed, but fresh and provocative in the engagement it offers. What Macaulay essayed was all too readily accepted, and then all too readily swept aside; his demonstrable errors became means of dismissing what should have been seen as stimuli. His success led many inferior practitioners to regurgitate his preoccupations until they became commonplace, but they were often brave pioneer work when he first wrestled with them. His own irony should haunt us: he still deserves attention for the way he tried to think about historical questions whether or not the world has since gone somewhere else. Apart from any other consideration, he never lost sight of his duty as an entertainer, and we have lost a great deal if history can no longer entertain.

4 The History of England

This work is for the present over. On Friday next, the 1st of December, we publish. I hardly know what to anticipate. Every body who has seen the book, that is to say, Lord Jeffrey, Ellis, Trevelyan, Hannah, and Longman, predict complete success, and say that it is as entertaining as a novel. But the truth is that, in such a case, friends are not to be trusted, and booksellers, after they have struck a bargain, are even less to be trusted than friends. The partiality of an author for what he has written is nothing compared to the partiality of a publisher for what he has bought. However a few weeks will show.

Macaulay to his brother Charles,
27 November 1848 (*Letters*, IV, 382)

The History of England from the Accession of James the Second as published in 1848 and 1855 (with the posthumous additions of 1861) covers a very short period in enormous detail, but its composition was overshadowed by Macaulay's dreams of writing the history of centuries. There was the history he had devised with Ellis in 1828 for the Society for the Diffusion of Useful Knowledge in which he was to cover English history from the Union of Crowns in 1603 to the ouster of James II in 1688; there was the history he had outlined to Napier in 1838 on receiving the Mackintosh collection in which he intended to go from the Revolution (but apparently without proposing to include the reign of James) down to 1832. Macaulay was not conscious of being a Whig historian – the term was reserved for definition and elaboration by future generations – but he was much aware of being a Whig who wanted to write a great history. Therefore he was aware of those his audience would see as his Tory competitors: David Hume's volumes of the

1750s had covered the seventeenth century up to 1688, and were followed by his narratives of Tudor and medieval times; in the 1820s the Roman Catholic John Lingard began his *History of England* in Roman times and would reach the Revolution; Macaulay's friend Mahon, Whig in bias but Tory in affiliation – so his literary success would be marked as another Tory laurel – was engaged on covering the eighteenth century; Sir Archibald Alison, the Scots Tory who would succeed Macaulay as Lord Rector of the University of Glasgow, wrote ten volumes on the *History of Europe*, published between 1833 and 1842. Macaulay's *History of England* would deal with far fewer years than any of them, but in readership and influence it would beat them all. The Whigs had a victory, inasmuch as Macaulay was a Whig. But in the event that hardly seemed to matter. Politically, the break-up of the Tories in 1846 meant that at Macaulay's death in 1859 his Tory ideological adversary of 1839, Gladstone, was Chancellor of the Exchequer under Palmerston, the most congenial to Macaulay in policy among his colleagues in the Whig cabinets of 1839–41 and 1846–8. The *History* was not acclaimed as a Whig victory, but as what Macaulay valued infinitely more, an English victory. It attracted numerous critics from the outset, but initially not on a party basis: ideological opposition to him came from obvious areas outside regular party channels, vehemently from neo-Jacobites, Carlyleans, Irish nationalists, more mildly from Roman Catholics. Its most obvious Tory adversaries would be High Churchmen, among them a cousin of his own, the Rev. Churchill Babington, but their outrage was more clerical than Tory and Macaulay's hostility to their historical antecedents stemmed from Zachary's influence even more than from Whig party sentiment.

Macaulay may have been somewhat surprised at the main body of his *History's* being so loudly applauded across party lines, and he was certainly gratified at the generosity of predictable adversaries: the Reverend Dr Charles Russell of Maynooth in the *Dublin Review* (June 1849) was 'not unhandsome', he thought, 'nor, for Roman Catholics, unfair'. An old personal enemy like John Wilson Croker in the *Quarterly Review* he expected to be ineffectively venomous, in which anticipation he was also gratified. Nor was he surprised when the Prime Minister, Lord John Russell, found his criticism of the old Whigs unpleasing: 'It is natural that a Russell should be partial to the Exclusionists,' he assured him on 3 January

1849, amused as always at the absurdity of self-identification with illustrious ancestors. In the years of his apprenticeship he had shown himself a keen critic of Tory historians who had dragged their present-day political prejudices into their writing, and in the leading journal of Whig ideology had preached against such propensities. He had written to Mahon on 31 December 1836 in affectionate criticism, but still in censure, of the tendency in Mahon's *History of England*:

> The practice of seasoning history with those pungent observations which elicit cheers in the House of Commons is, I think, very injudicious in a writer who aspires to more than a month's popularity. It is a practice which heightens the temporary effect of a book, but which greatly detracts from its permanent value.

He had publicly been more severe on Thomas Peregrine Courtenay, Sir William Temple's Tory biographer and editor, for such solecisms (*Edinburgh*, October 1838):

> Not only are these passages out of place in a historical work, but some of them are intrinsically such that they would become the editor of a third-rate party newspaper better than a gentleman of Mr Courtenay's talents and knowledge. For example we are told that, 'it is a remarkable circumstance, familiar to those who are acquainted with history, but suppressed by the new Whigs, that the liberal politicians of the seventeenth century and the greater part of the eighteenth, never extended their liberality to the native Irish, or the professors of the ancient religion'. What schoolboy of fourteen is ignorant of this remarkable circumstance? What Whig, new or old, was ever such an idiot as to think that it could be suppressed?

At least his own limits were clear for him.

Macaulay may have been contentious in his manner of asserting consensus, but he consciously sought the consensus he obtained. He had always recognized what little basic difference now existed between Whig and Tory views of 1688. David Hume, defender of the early Stuarts, declared of the Revolution in the last pages of his *History of England*:

By deciding many important questions in favour of liberty, and still more by that great precedent of deposing one king, and establishing a new family, it gave such an ascendant to popular principles, as has put the nature of the English constitution beyond all controversy. And it may justly be affirmed, without any danger of exaggeration, that we, in this island, have ever since enjoyed, if not the best system of government, at least the most entire system of liberty, that ever was known amongst mankind.

Macaulay must have smiled at Hume's assertion that the nature of the English constitution was beyond all controversy, but with its broader meaning he agreed; he himself asserted the Reform Act of 1832 to be the logical culmination of progress from the 1688 Settlement. From the time of Hume onwards the area of historiographical agreement on the Revolution had grown even wider. Dalrymple's revelations on Whig dealings with Louis XIV both before and after the Revolution should have made impossible the parading of party saints as a title to particular glory. But the publication of the fragments of Fox and Mackintosh on the reign of James II and the Revolution meant that Macaulay was doing nothing new in retelling the story as a modern Whig. So little was his main thesis open to party hostility that Alison gave the *History* a most generous welcome in *Blackwood's* and Croker, having combed the dump for hostile arguments, could only complain that Fox and Mackintosh had made Macaulay's *History* unnecessary.[83]

Yet the *History* was both courageous and controversial. It was revolutionary in its impact and extent: no work of history had ever meant so much to so many. Macaulay could hardly have reckoned on its incredible success, yet that was what he had sought. His audience became his greatest means of compensation for the loss of the companionship of Margaret and for the end of his arguments with Zachary. It is justly famous that he wrote to Napier on 5 November 1841: 'The materials for an amusing narrative are immense. I shall not be satisfied unless I produce something which shall for a few days supersede the last fashionable novel on the tables of young ladies.' It is less often considered how deeply this indicated his longing for its presence on the table of a young lady who would never see it. It was no male chauvinist statement of ambition to reach the ultimate in readership: psychologically he wanted women readers more than men. What he thought would interest women may perhaps best be seen in his assessment of a woman's achievement (*Edinburgh*, January 1843):

> Jane Austen ... has given us a multitude of characters, all, in a certain sense, commonplace, all such as we meet every day. Yet they are all as perfectly discriminated from each other as if they were the most eccentric of human beings. There are, for example, four clergymen, none of whom we should be surprised to find in any parsonage in the kingdom, Mr Edward Ferrars, Mr Henry Tilney, Mr Edmund Bertram, and Mr Elton. They are all specimens of the upper part of the middle class. They have all been liberally educated. They all lie under the restraints of the same sacred profession. They are all young. They are all in love. Not one of them has any hobbyhorse, to use the phrase of Sterne. Not one has a ruling passion, such as we read of in Pope. Who would not have expected them to be insipid likenesses of each other? No such thing. Harpagon is not more unlike to Jourdain, Joseph Surface is not more unlike to Sir Lucius O'Trigger, than every one of Miss Austen's young divines to all his reverend brethren. And almost all this is done by touches so delicate, that they elude analysis, that they defy the powers of description, and that we know them to exist only by the general effect to which they have contributed.

He would have wished his *History* to inspire further achievements by women in history and literature, among them his niece Baba (who would write Zachary's biography half a century later); he would be mindful of such women as Sarah Austin, whose translation of Ranke's *History of the Popes* he had reviewed with such enthusiasm.[84]

He did not preoccupy himself with the latest novels which he hoped his *History* might temporarily oust. In the 1820s and early 1830s he had loved reading novels with Hannah and Margaret, and talking nonsense about them; and therefore he had no interest in them now. That his immediate competitors included Currer, Ellis and Acton Bell (in private life the Brontë sisters) is instructive: the readers who first devoured the *History* included some who had welcomed *Wuthering Heights* and *The Tenant of Wildfell Hall* the same year, and more who had delighted in *Jane Eyre* the year before; we may even amuse ourselves by noticing that Macaulay's William III, derided for his lack of social graces and courtly manners, becomes as impressive a study in the misunderstood hero as is Mr Rochester. But the association is limited to the common readership, and the common cultural roots. Macaulay had been very amusing in his essay on Byron, describing Byron's perpetual incarnation in the same misunderstood and outwardly repellent hero, but here, as with much else of Byron, there was admiration within Macaulay's mockery. With the assistance of William himself and the contemporary sources, Macaulay made a much better Byronic hero of William (at certain moments) than Byron had ever created. Dickens he liked and generally admired, and Thackeray he came to consider the greatest novelist of his day. But none of their works seems to have influenced him beyond obvious points of inspiration from their common source in Scott. He read his old friend Lytton – a best-selling novelist by now – with some pleasure, but any literary influence had been from Macaulay, not on him. When the *History*, the *Lays* and the *Essays* were conquering their thousands and their tens of thousands, Macaulay wrote to Ellis on 9 March 1850:

It is odd that the last twenty-five years which have witnessed the greatest progress ever made in physical science, the greatest victories ever achieved by man over matter, should have produced hardly a volume that will be remembered in 1900, and should have seen the breed of great advocates and parliamentary orators become extinct among us.

He went to the past for his ideas on the art of historical writing, whether he chose to take them from historians, dramatists, novelists or poets.[85]

Macaulay believed that history was a branch of literature, that its sources and content should include all branches of literature, and that it should be presented with the techniques in depicting human society and individual character which literature, in its fictional form, had achieved. In May 1828 the *Edinburgh* published his essay on history. He did not reprint it in *Critical and Historical Essays*, partly perhaps because by 1843 he doubted whether he could hope to reach the heights it demanded. But it largely remained his creed, and for all the inability of his *History* to come up fully to his wishes, and for all the early crudities in which he expressed their resolution, it remains essential if we are to understand both the *History* and the primary cause of its success:

> The perfect historian is he in whose work the character and spirit
> of an age is exhibited in miniature. He relates no fact, he attributes
> no expression to his characters, which is not authenticated by
> sufficient testimony. But, by judicious selection, rejection, and
> arrangement, he gives to truth those attractions which have been
> usurped by fiction. In his narrative a due subordination is
> observed: some transactions are prominent; others retire. But
> the scale on which he represents them is increased or diminished,
> not according to the dignity of persons concerned in them, but
> according to the degree in which they elucidate the condition
> of society and the nature of man. He shows us the court, the
> camp, and the senate. But he shows us also the nation. He con-
> siders no anecdote, no peculiarity of manner, no familiar saying,
> as too insignificant for his notice which is not too insignificant
> to illustrate the operation of laws, of religion, and of education,
> and to mark the progress of the human mind. Men will not merely
> be described, but will be made intimately known to us. The
> changes of manners will be indicated, not merely by a few general
> phrases or a few extracts from statistical documents, but by
> appropriate images presented in every line.

What the novels of Scott had achieved in rescuing the history of
Scottish society from oblivion established the agenda for Macaulay's
ideal historian in 1828:

> If a man, such as we are supposing, should write the history
> of England, he would assuredly not omit the battles, the sieges,
> the negotiations, the seditions, the ministerial changes. But with
> these he would intersperse the details which are the charm of
> historical romances. At Lincoln Cathedral there is a beautiful
> painted window, which was made by an apprentice out of the
> pieces of glass which had been rejected by his master. It is so
> far the superior to every other in the church, that, according
> to the tradition, the vanquished artist killed himself from mortifi-
> cation. Sir Walter Scott, in the same manner, has used those
> fragments of truth which historians have scornfully thrown
> behind them in a manner which may well excite their envy. He
> has constructed out of their gleanings works which, even

considered as histories, are scarcely less valuable than theirs. But a truly great historian would reclaim those materials which the novelist has appropriated. The history of the government, and the history of the people, would be exhibited in that mode in which alone they can be exhibited justly, in inseparable conjunction and intermixture. We should not then have to look for the wars and votes of the Puritans in Clarendon, and for their phraseology in Old Mortality; for one half of King James in Hume, and for the other half in the Fortunes of Nigel.

At the close of the essay he acknowledged that such a historian was less likely to arrive than another Shakespeare or another Homer; and his idea of the inevitable decline of poetry with progress meant that another Shakespeare or another Homer was an impossibility.

Yet, having stated his agenda, his first thought was to fulfil it himself. Within the next few months he had sketched out to Ellis his proposal for his history of England under the Stuarts, and as Ellis reported to Henry Brougham on 14 September 1828:

He proposes to begin with an introductory view of the state in which society and opinions were at the death of Elizabeth. In the body of the history, he intends to introduce, wherever he can do so with perfect security as to truth, characteristic anecdotes and speeches – giving for instance King James's broad Scotch verbatim.[86]

The *History* whose publication began in 1848 did not take this last risk, for the very good reason that Macaulay came to realize how few of the sounds of the past had survived. Scott was a bad exemplar here: his dependence on oral evidence meant that his use of the Scots language rested on the form in which he heard it, but even the most punctilious inheritors of folk narratives and folk ballads were not proof against adulteration of material, to say nothing of intonation and vocabulary. When it came to writing *Ivanhoe* Scott made Gurth and Wamba 'talk like nothing on earth', as G.M. Young remarked. So far as may be gathered from his letters Macaulay could imitate contemporary Scots well (how Scots did Zachary sound, especially in moments of excitement?), but the Scottish speech had changed since James I. The problem existed even more acutely with William III. Macaulay's William was a hero, albeit a hero presented with far more humour than Mr Rochester could have sustained: in detail, he was misunderstood by Englishmen more as Jane Austen's Emma misunderstood Mr Knightley. And William's situation interdicted the idea of speech reproduction:

> One misfortune, which was imputed to him as a crime, was his bad English. He spoke our language, but not well. His accent was foreign: his diction was inelegant: and his vocabulary seems to have been no larger than was necessary for the transaction of business. To the difficulty which he felt in expressing himself, and to his consciousness that his pronunciation was bad, must be partly ascribed the taciturnity and the short answers which gave so much offence. Our literature he was incapable of enjoying or of understanding. He never once, during his whole reign, showed himself at the theatre. The poets who wrote Pindaric verses in his praise, complained that their flights of sublimity were beyond his comprehension. Those who are acquainted with the panegyrical odes of that age will perhaps be of opinion that he did not lose much by his ignorance.

The alien and unpopular 'deliverer' could sustain his dignity with such a description; he would hardly have been proof against an attempt to reproduce his bad English. Macaulay's repression of his own partly alien status expressed itself here with constructive sympathy, a strong moral improvement on what he thought of doing with James I, the effect of which would have been to increase English intoxication with stage Scotsmen. William's writing was in Dutch or French, which made nonsense of the whole idea of reproducing his actual speech. Macaulay's *History* was free enough with quotations in Latin, Spanish, German, French, Italian and Dutch in the footnotes, but in his text he gave up the search for authenticity, however ersatz, and rendered documentary evidence into modern summary sometimes phrased colloquially. For this process he would use inverted commas, apparently with no intention of leading the reader to assume the statements quoted were more than the sense of what was said. But it was a concession to his general audience which marked a radical departure from his original ideas. The idea of making the past speak for itself became the practice of making it speak through him.[87]

His contempt for James Boswell as a man he made stand in inverse proportion to his veneration for James Boswell as a biographer. He had written in the *Edinburgh* for September 1831:

> Homer is not more decidedly the first of heroic poets, Shakspeare is not more decidedly the first of dramatists, Demosthenes is not more decidedly the first of orators, than Boswell is the first of biographers. He has no second. He has distanced all his competitors so decidedly that it is not worth while to place them. Eclipse is first, and the rest nowhere.

The essay on history regrets that Clarendon had not:

> condescended to be the Boswell of the Long Parliament.... Let us suppose that he had made his Cavaliers and Roundheads talk in their own style; that he had reported some of the ribaldry of Rupert's pages, and some of the cant of Harrison and Fleetwood. Would not his work in that case have been more interesting? Would it not have been more accurate?

But Clarendon and Boswell had been witnesses to the events and persons they had described best. For all of his belief in time travel, Macaulay could never quite duplicate their advantages. What he did do was consider the element in Boswell's success, his teasing out of Johnson's opinions on all subjects, his readiness to tell stories with no decent regard to the susceptibilities of Hannah More or anyone else, his insistence on blurting out anything of interest with no apparent concern for the figure he might cut in admitting it, his capacity for presenting his subject in absolutely vivid detail. As Macaulay wrote in his biography of Johnson for Black's *Britannica* in 1856:

> Boswell's book has done for him more than the best of his own books could do. The memory of other authors is kept alive by their own works. But the memory of Johnson keeps many of his works alive. The old philosopher is still among us in the brown coat with the metal buttons and the shirt which ought to be at wash, blinking, puffing, rolling his head, drumming with his fingers, tearing his meat like a tiger, and swallowing his tea in

oceans. No human being who has been more than seventy years in the grave is so well known as he.

Macaulay's *History* is a perpetual attempt to tease out the England, Scotland and Ireland of 1685–1700 into a comparable vividness. His models of excellence here – for Thucydides to him was 'the first' of historians no less than Boswell of biographers – put him at a disadvantage. Their contemporaneity with their subjects doomed him to some degree of failure from the start. But he took Boswell's capacity for self-degradation and applied it to historical sources, stressing that he had to examine lampoons, satires, scurrilous pamphlets, journals of worthless voluptuaries, contemptible and half-lunatic theological scribblings, bad verses and worse plays. At the beginning of the *History* he reasserted that part of the work of his ideal historian imagined twenty years earlier:

> It will be my endeavour to relate the history of the people as well as the history of the government, to trace the progress of useful and ornamental arts, to describe the rise of religious sects and the changes of literary taste, to portray the manners of successive generations, and not to pass by with neglect even the revolutions which have taken place in dress, furniture, repasts, and public amusements. I shall cheerfully bear the reproach of having descended below the dignity of history, if I can succeed in placing before the English of the nineteenth century a true picture of the life of their ancestors.

In so doing, he was condemned for trivialization by writers as various as the vengeful Croker and the judicious Lingard. His readers seem to have loved it, and by his extension of history's concerns he extended its audience. The urgency of his crusade was well expressed in the essay on history: 'We have read books called Histories of England, under the reign of George the Second, in which the rise of Methodism is not even mentioned.' So successful was he that his achievement has been taken for granted by later generations, and, as he foresaw, he has been ridiculed by scholars whose occupation he created. With little evident anxiety on this score, he took pleasure in occasionally showing himself in the text of his own *History* at work in the more disreputable sources of the hitherto neglected human past, such as on the effects of the French war in 1692:

There was much suffering and much repining. In some counties mobs attacked the granaries. An idle man of wit and pleasure, who little thought that his buffoonery would ever be cited to illustrate the history of his times, complained that, in this year, wine ceased to be put on many hospitable tables where he had been accustomed to see it, and that its place was supplied by punch.

What Macaulay was not prepared to do was to sacrifice his standing as bard and teacher, as Boswell had. The *History* is written with an eye to the future more than to the present, and the author remains perpetually before the reader's eyes less as a judge of what he describes than as a guide to his audience's ethical responses. The *History* being intended to train a citizenry for participation in and possession of a future England, its author was vigilant in his desire to save the future masters from error. It says much for Macaulay's humour and resources that he so seldom becomes sanctimonious in the process: he evangelized as taught by Zachary, but also as one who knew how difficult it could be being taught by Zachary. The tension within him induced his censure for Horace Walpole's luxuriating in the entertainment he was giving and, one must infer, his own similar propensity; yet he perpetually enhanced edification with his seductive and almost conspiratorial style. He owed more to Boswell and Walpole than he could fully admit.[88]

Macaulay's use of social history operated in two separate ways: he introduced it constantly at almost any opportunity into the narrative of main events, frequently in conjunction with political developments, sometimes in a quick aside, sometimes in the strong setting of a scene; and he devoted his third chapter to the state of England in 1685, much as Ellis had told Brougham in 1828 he intended to do for England in 1603. The first excited flickers of irritation in his own time, but no sensible historian would ignore his example today. It is the third chapter which excites reproach. Because its reporting on population, commerce, agriculture, manufactures, religion, professional codes, revenue, army, navy, daily life among country gentry, clergy, yeomanry, townsfolk, means of transport and so forth, was entirely unprecedented, it clearly suffers by comparison with modern findings. But this is to approach it from the wrong end: the wonder of the thing is to see what one man could do at the dawn of modern historiography. The usual charge that

Macaulay's *History* distorted the past by adverse comparison with
the present might seem to have ammunition here, especially given
the derisive conclusion to that chapter ('Delusion which leads Men
to overrate the Happiness of preceding Generations'), although he
ends by mocking the thought that the mirage-like Golden Age his
contemporaries saw in the past would be applied by posterity to
his own time:

> It is now the fashion to place the golden age of England in times
> when noblemen were destitute of comforts the want of which
> would be intolerable to a modern footman, when farmers and
> shopkeepers breakfasted on loaves the very sight of which would
> raise a riot in a modern workhouse, when to have a clean shirt
> once a week was a privilege reserved for the higher class of gentry,
> when men died faster in the lanes of our towns than they now
> die on the coast of Guiana.

And he conjectured that in the twentieth century, while progress
might enable workers to have meat each day, and medicine might
prolong life, and comforts and luxuries might be available to every
wage-earner,

> it may then be the mode to assert that the increase of wealth
> and the progress of science have benefited the few at the expense
> of the many, and to talk of the reign of Queen Victoria as the
> time when England was truly merry England, when all classes
> were bound together by brotherly sympathy, when the rich did
> not grind the faces of the poor, and when the poor did not envy
> the splendour of the rich.

That such nonsense is not talked nowadays – save in high places
– we owe to Macaulay and Marx, whose views of material progress
somewhat resembled one another, however violently they differed
on the desirabilities of class interrelationships within the stages of
that progress. But it is fair to say that Macaulay's idea of progress
was most strongly grounded on the advance of medical science and
on the diminution of human cruelty. He had a personal physical
horror of beholding suffering, and as he looked back to the past
he was perpetually conscious of the omnipresence of burnings, dis-
embowellings, tortures, mutilations, executions. Progress was much

more urgent in his mind, because of his sense of the incredible speed of material improvement and conditions of life in his own paternal ancestry, and if he stressed the filth, squalor, murders, burnings and hideous personal acts of vengeance in Highland society when he reached that part of his *History*, it was with a clear sense of how narrowly he had escaped it by but a few generations. He wrote with particular distaste for the physical toil thrust upon women in seventeenth-century Highland Scotland, and the readiness of the men to assume that it was their right and duty to leave women the heavy work: this was to think of the back-breaking, dung-bespattered daily grind which had been the portion of Hannahs and Margarets less than a century since. His use of his contemporary England as a yardstick against which to judge 1685 was sensible in view of his anxiety to educate his audience: if they were to see 1685 it was natural that they should look at it first from their own time. He was thinking not of future academic historians but of readers with little or no awareness of the past, especially the socio-economic past; and, however crudely, he got some sense of it across to them.

But the third chapter made for generalizations, most notably with respect to social and ideological interest-groups, and it conflicts with the individual portraits of men in those groups as they appear in their own right throughout the narrative of his *History*. Let us look at the example Macaulay chose from Jane Austen: her clergymen. Professor Jane Millgate rightly contrasts his admiration for the Austen clerics with the somewhat caricaturish version of the Anglican clergy in 1685 (and beyond) which Macaulay presents in Chapter Three. But Jane Austen is not his guide in his remarks on the clergy in Chapter Three, unless it be through Mr Collins in *Pride and Prejudice*, the servile cleric cringingly dependent on his bullying patron, and the one notable Austen clergyman whom Macaulay does not mention in his tribute to her. (No doubt he excluded Mr Collins as he has some points in common with the later Mr Elton, of *Emma*, and Macaulay wanted to stress Jane Austen's capacity for delicacy in differentiation. But Mr Elton is character where Mr Collins is caricature.) Macaulay's third chapter is obliged to take a panoramic view on all questions. His contemporary sources on the clergy were unflattering, and often anti-clerical; his evidence was sparse; he succumbed naturally to the attractions of vivid portraiture in novels and plays; he would rightly have been influenced by the deferential rural clergymen presented in Addison's *Spectator*; he would have been affected by his revulsion for all forms of patronage and by his father's hostility to parsons whose theology was dictated by their stipend. He may not have been so very wrong, but he was crude, and comic.

Once he is dealing with individual clergymen who play a part in his *History*, even though they may have but a few lines in a few scenes, the method alters. The generalization with which he had pronounced his judgments in the essay on Hallam is as far from him as the generalization with which he summed up the occupation-groups of Chapter Three. In the enormous cast of characters under his scrutiny he made such clergymen as Thomas Ken, John Tillotson, Henry Compton, William Sancroft, William Sherlock, Jeremy Collier and above all Gilbert Burnet become figures as vital for their discoverers in his pages as Jane Austen's divines: in Ken, who comforted the beaten Monmouth rebels, went to the Tower as one of the Seven Bishops defying James, and was ousted from the See of Bath and Wells for his refusal to take the oaths to William and Mary in violation of his oath to James, Macaulay drew one of the most difficult of all portraits, that of a supremely lovable saint. The courage, disingenuousness and pride of Compton; the forthright and learned piety of Tillotson; the mingled principle and pedantry of Sancroft; the cool effrontery of Sherlock; the lonely moral crusade of Collier – all become as familiar as Edmund Bertram's high-principled devotion. Burnet, the restless, intriguing, brave, indiscreet, devoted, egregious Williamite (and Marian) partisan is drawn more fully than any; with the advantage of his own extensive narrative of his times, he becomes a natural readers' favourite, deployed with critical affection. With Sancroft alone is there a serious want of sympathy.

Macaulay's portraits of individuals would invite, and frequently receive, indignant objurgation; some of it was justified. Apart from the boldness with which he forced his view of his characters on his audience, so vast an array was bound to provoke individual dissents. But it could not be said that Macaulay divided them politically, granting favour if they supported the Revolution and obloquy if they opposed it. He clearly regretted that so fine a man as Ken refused to take the oath to William and Mary, but his Ken remains a saint to the end. (In the same way he naturally supported the English Reformation, but had a far higher estimate of John Fisher

and Thomas More than of any of its makers or even martyrs.)
On the Revolution, Compton had the credentials of a zealous Protestant Bishop of London who played a part in its accomplishment
from the first, but Macaulay found him dishonest in his dealings
with James II and snobbishly arrogant in his attempts to gain Canter-
bury in preference to Tillotson. Nor is it a matter of practical against
woolly-minded clerics: Macaulay succeeded in presenting nice distinctions between practicality and worldliness, on the one hand,
and sanctity and pedantry, on the other. Macaulay is not known
for any personal religious beliefs at this time (which simply means
that he kept them to himself, whatever they were, not that he had
none) and he is well known to have disliked metaphysical specula-
tion. But he was personally fascinated by religious literature, and
examined its rhetoric, vagaries of creed, logical inconsistencies, ratio
of cant to piety, sense of personal advancement or aggrandizement,
indication of devotional conviction, propensity to impossible human
demands, content of sectarian hatred, ethical pastorate and even
mystical quality, all with the insights he had learned from his father
and a coolness in scientific analysis occasionally – though not generally – warped by his high sense of the ridiculous. Tillotson's sermons
he held in the utmost regard, despite the fact that he was hardly
likely to have been profoundly sympathetic to their author's interest
in whether Lucifer might conceivably obtain salvation (as Macaulay
regretfully recorded, Tillotson was less sanguine about Roman Catholics).

The third chapter of the *History* also shows signs that, for all
his brave announcement in the first chapter that he would go forward to 1832, he had doubts as to whether he would last long
enough to produce another panorama of England in, say 1745,
or, if he preferred, to show individual changes in its institutions
by that date. His ribald description of the habits of the squirearchy in
1685 avowedly owed something to the mid-eighteenth-century novels
of Henry Fielding. In part the problem was that the great pioneer
chapter demanded a static treatment, and what Professor John Clive
has so well termed 'the propulsive capacity of his imagination' gave
him a natural incentive to keep his narrative moving. Nor, despite
his wish to give the history of the people, would the people have
enough to do in the crowded chronology which was to follow;
hence his description of the Court and capital related more specifically to 1685 than did his account of the other cities and the country.

The difficulty was less one of staying out of his own century than of staying out of its predecessor. He was itching to write portions of the *History* he would never produce, and while this did not produce much anachronism in his narrative of events, it would affect his discussion of pure social history. On the other hand, in the third chapter, and more particularly later when dealing with the abolition of censorship and the birth of newspapers, he was supreme in showing the importance of communications, the dissemination of the printed word, the extension of commonplace human understanding, and the ironies of legislation receiving little thought yet productive of what he rightly termed a 'great revolution'. He may be pardoned for describing the emergence of an unlicensed press in 1695 as 'events which no preceding historian has condescended to mention, but which were of far greater importance than the achievements of William's army or Russell's fleet'.[89]

The problems of a static subject in the third chapter were partly offset by its placement after the tremendous sweep of the first chapter, moving from the dawn of English history to 1660, and the convulsive treatment of the second, which had to take full responsibility for the twenty-five years of Charles II's reign, ten years more than would be covered in the twenty-three further chapters that he would write. The scheme gave the reader a necessary chance to draw breath. The use Macaulay made in the third chapter of discussion of problems of transport supplied a vital background for considerations he wished to be borne firmly in mind for what would follow, and at the same time the pace with which the reader was moved around the country kept the energy flowing. He would return to the theme of communications difficulties appropriately and happily from time to time, in his *History*, for example when he came to describe the 'bold and crafty attempt' of the Whigs at the beginning of 1690 to produce in the Corporation Bill a law which would strip the Tories of their political influence, a measure Macaulay made it clear he thought unwise and dishonest. Its proponents took advantage of the Tories' absence at Yuletide festivities:

> the general opinion at first was that the Whigs would win the day. But it soon became clear that the fight would be a hard one. The mails had carried out along all the high roads the tidings that, on the second of January, the Commons had agreed to a retrospective penal law against the whole Tory party, and that,

on the tenth, that law would be considered for the last time. The whole kingdom was moved from Northumberland to Cornwall. A hundred knights and squires left their halls hung with mistletoe and holly, and their boards groaning with brawn and plum porridge, and rode up post to town, cursing the short days, the cold weather, the miry roads, and the villainous Whigs.   [The Tories won.][90]

Macaulay apportioned his introductory matter so unevenly as against the main text in order to set the political scene and its antecedents, but by doing so he made difficulties for the remainder of the *History*. It has curious reminiscences of his master Scott's frequent need for introductory matter which makes many of the novels slow to take off. Macaulay had little difficulty in keeping any narrative moving, but his anxiety to instruct a public which he recognized as often only dimly aware of historical developments meant that he had, after all, to provide a seventeenth-century narrative, but one with much more unsatisfactory proportions than those in which he had originally shaped his intended history, back in 1828 and in subsequent essays. In his first chapter he dealt thematically with medieval history, glanced at the Reformation, and gave some detail to the conflicts between the early Stuarts and their enemies. We shall return to its implications on the theme of revolution; suffice it to say that it proved the really contentious section of the *History* in the eyes of contemporary critics. The otherwise laudatory Alison waxed lyrical with horror on Macaulay's impiety towards Charles I, and his aggrandizement of the Commonwealth.

The second chapter ranging from 1660 to 1685 made for more subtle dangers, and they were less easy to separate from the main text. Macaulay had to introduce characters and issues which would continue to dominate the reign of James II and in some respects that of William and Mary. His exemplars in fiction and history gave him little help. Homer leaps into the *Iliad* with little discussion of its exceedingly complex preliminary history. Thucydides had a theme of war to whose outbreak all preliminary matter could be subordinated. Boswell had Johnson's early life as the obvious contour to precede the major work recounting their association. Novelists could summarize all they wished before letting their main work come into focus at its appropriate time. Macaulay was limited by the Mackintosh collection, whose abundance on the reign of James led him to go over ground commenced by Fox and largely surveyed by Mackintosh. The *History* did contain much primary material from 1680. Macaulay had decided that only a full discussion of James's reign would make sense of the Revolution, but it would distance him too drastically from his ideal commencement in 1688 were he to move in detail through the anti-Catholic hysteria induced by the perjuries of Titus Oates in 1679, and the subsequent revenge of Charles II against the Whigs when the Rye House Plot of their extremists was discovered. Both of these events were therefore treated dramatically but briefly: yet both profoundly affected what would occur during James's reign and the Revolution. On the whole Macaulay proved both effective and instructive in presenting Oates himself and in laying a foundation for the comparable methods which like-minded perjurers would employ during William's reign, but he made somewhat less of the degree to which so many individuals who would play a part in the Revolution had assisted the persecution of the Catholics. The Rye House Plot he covered very rapidly, and his subsequent references to it seem almost to exculpate persons who had been implicated in it. More was involved than considerations of space. It is perhaps the one point where he was a little solicitous of Whig party sentiment, and even there his strictures on Whig factionalism, fury and folly moved the reproach of his Prime Minister.

More seriously, Macaulay was anxious to present the Revolution as a major event in the advance of human liberty, and therefore wished to diminish the prevalent Tory notion that it was above all bound up with hatred of Catholicism. When in his main text he directly confronted evidence for the anti-Catholic impulse he faced it, discussed it and usually blamed James II for it. But obliquely he managed to imply that the deep-seated anti-Catholic sentiment was not in itself the dominant factor. In so doing he managed to carry Tories with him: after all, Catholic Emancipation was now a thing of the past, and he himself was the last major British political martyr on a specifically Catholic issue. This consideration also swayed him: he preferred to think that he had been defeated by an electoral collapse into bigotry which would not last. He reaffirmed his own readiness to court unpopularity by stressing in the first chapter how important the role of medieval Roman Catholicism had been in advancing social equality. Had he commenced his detailed narrative in 1679 he would have been in danger of presenting anti-Catholicism as a British institution, and it was one British institution he had given his political life to eradicate. The last thing he wished to do was to give it a new lease of life by over-stressing its historical significance. (He made no attempt to diminish its significance for Ireland, but he tied it very much to racial hostility there.) Hence his *History* made much of the foolish king who sought to aggrandize Catholicism at the expense of English liberties, and something of the wise pope who sought to restrain him.[91]

The success of the *History* above all rested on the interest of its characters, and here the second chapter was also a mixed blessing. If certain characters, above all James II himself, suffered from insufficient discussion of their earlier lives during Charles's reign – Macaulay distorted his own portrait of James from the outset by making nothing of his unquestionable skill as a naval commander under Charles – the second chapter subordinated them further in being necessarily dominated by Charles II himself. The portrait of Charles there, the account of his death which begins the main text in Chapter Four, and the flashback references contrasting him with James and William, are a startling achievement. It was a fine proof of what Macaulay could do with his material, and what his material could do with him. Directly, his Charles is a cold, cynical, charming, utterly worthless voluptuary who bartered his kingdom into vassalage to Louis XIV: what Macaulay could not do, however much he tried – and he tried – was to kill his delight in the reprobate. His deeply reluctant and constantly stifled affection is a much more remarkable testimony to Charles's powers than any later attempts at rehabilitation could be. The classic revelation comes at the one event in Charles's life which receives detailed treatment from Macaulay, the hour of his death. The account of the death itself is pre-eminently concerned with Charles's reception into the Roman Catholic Church; and, with an oblique sympathy for both king and religion Macaulay would never own to directly, it is done with humanity and dignity. Nothing could be farther from the snarl in the Mackintosh essay, 'he died at last with the Host sticking in his throat.' The *History*'s account concludes:

The morning light began to peep through the windows of Whitehall; and Charles desired the attendants to pull aside the curtains, that he might have one more look at the day. He remarked that it was time to wind up a clock which stood near his bed. These little circumstances were long remembered, because they proved beyond dispute that, when he declared himself a Roman Catholic, he was in full possession of his faculties. He apologised to those who had stood round him all night for the trouble which he had caused. He had been, he said, a most unconscionable time dying; but he hoped they would excuse it. This was the last glimpse of that exquisite urbanity so often found potent to charm away the resentment of a justly incensed nation. . . .

Macaulay's account of the last words has become immortal. Lady Antonia Fraser has pointed out that Charles did not, in fact, use the word 'unconscionable', but so deeply had Macaulay entered into a fleeting identification with the dying king that he has the squire's honour of sharpening Charles's last shaft of wit. He had not intended to mislead, but simply to convey his sense of what the last words meant. But posterity ascribed 'unconscionable' to Charles thereafter.

As James was to prove, Charles was not an easy act to follow, and the *History* takes a few pages to gather momentum once more. Characters already depicted with quick strokes are now to reappear under much more detailed examination, and yet sometimes inhibited by having made their initial entrance in summary. The Whigs are still under the shadow of the recently deceased Shaftesbury, briefly but ferociously exhibited in the second chapter with much of the demonic character ascribed to him in Dryden's 'Absalom and Achitophel': in fact he is one of the few men whose escape from capital punishment Macaulay regretted. Subsequent historians would argue that by setting up his characters in advance, Macaulay showed his imposition of existing prejudices on his material. There is something in this, but much less than its proponents imagine. Macaulay's researches throughout the 1840s had continued steadily, and he seems to have written and rewritten consistently during that time: he told Napier on 20 July 1842 that he had written something less than half a volume 'rough-hewn', he told him on 20 October 1843 that he had 'got into the midst of the stream with my history', he told Hannah on 5 October 1846 that 'The last paragraph which I wrote could not have been written without the Journals of the House of Lords, [Louis' Ambassador to James] Barillon's despatches in manuscript, the London Gazettes for 1687'; and yet on 17 July

1848 he and Ellis were desperately struggling with problems of the number of burials in Leeds in 1685, as raw as material could be for the third chapter.

Artistically, he held back some of the strongest effects in his text until the time was ripe. His full presentation of Marlborough as the great Satanic genius bursts like a thunderclap in the seventeenth chapter with his thesis, conjecturing

> that this wise, brave, wicked man, was meditating a plan worthy of his fertile intellect and daring spirit, and not less worthy of his deeply corrupted heart, a plan which, if it had not been frustrated by strange means, would have ruined William without benefiting James, and would have made the successful traitor master of England and arbiter of Europe.

Hitherto Marlborough (then plain Churchill) was but one of a number of perjured conspirators against James, distinguished by his personal obligations, his political skill, and his wife's ascendancy over James's second daughter Anne; and then he was shown to be an outstanding commander in William's forces. The occasion for bringing on the suspicion of the grand doublecross was Marlborough's overtures to the exiled James, but where Macaulay had earlier shown him as simply a peculiarly disgraceful example of a treacherous and faithless age, he now took stock of his man in his own right. Macaulay could have left his portrait as it had been, pointing out how readily men took out insurance on their political futures by keeping themselves in some good odour with the present regime and with its predecessor and possible supplanter. This would no longer do him. Where possible, everyone must be shown as distinct from everyone else:

> Among those who were guilty of this wickedness three men stand pre-eminent, Russell, Godolphin, and Marlborough. No three men could be, in head and heart, more unlike to one another; and the peculiar qualities of each gave a peculiar quality to his villainy. The treason of Russell is to be attributed partly to fractiousness; the treason of Godolphin is to be attributed altogether to timidity; the treason of Marlborough was the treason of a man of great genius and boundless ambition.

Unless one adopts Sir Winston Churchill's comfortable solution in his life of his ancestor (accompanied by his assurance that history will not rest until she has fastened the label 'liar' on Macaulay's elegant (*sic*) coat-tail) that Marlborough's alleged treasonable Jacobite traffickings were imagined by Jacobite forgers, the distinctions make more sense than Macaulay's earlier simple, blanket solution.

Hugh Trevor-Roper, in introducing his Penguin abridgment of the *History*, quotes with approval S.R.Gardiner's pronouncement: Macaulay's 'judgment of a political situation was as superb as his judgment of personal character was weak'. But how could one be superb if the other were weak? Politics is about people. Winston Churchill and J.H.Plumb found that Macaulay's sexual inexperience made him incapable of judging character. We have not the slightest knowledge whether Macaulay did or did not have sexual experience, or if so, of what kind. He was an isolated student 'at the age when the passions are most impetuous and when levity is most pardonable' (as he said of Charles II among the Presbyterian Scots in 1650). He could not have had personal knowledge of what it means to be a lesbian, but he certainly showed he knew what he was talking about in discussing Anne's relationship with Marlborough's wife Sarah, and Marlborough's certainty of thereby controlling Anne's attitudes to her father James and her brother-in-law William. Macaulay vehemently denounced any suggestion that William III had sexual relations with his male favourites, but he presented with insight the love of Bentinck for William, his jealousy of Keppel, and the growing affections of William and Keppel. Macaulay wrote with all too deep an understanding of human grief on the death of loved ones, whether that of William for Mary, or of the Duchess of Portsmouth for Charles. His *History* simply gave him too few opportunities for showing his understanding of the human heart, and here again he could not live up to the fullness his essay on history had asked. But it is difficult to sustain the argument, however frequently repeated, that he gave his customers short shrift on character in place of what they would have obtained from their novels. It is idle to complain that his few, bold strokes of delineation, or his more subtle interweavings of further forms of revelation as his narrative proceeded, did less than justice to his innumerable figures: of course they were less than just. He was attempting to move a huge multitude, and exhibit their differentiation. Inevitably he had for the most part to be content with the facets most appropriate to his general narrative. His critics are his witness: he has been abused for portrait after portrait in language which assumes him to have built major biographies for each object of controversy. It was in keeping them in association with one another and yet retaining individual character-play that he did his work: naturally in literature as in life characters are impaired in their effectiveness by their fellows. The biography of single individuals gives a fuller play to their talents, but biography in its turn claims too much in human knowledge and is disproportionate in its obsessive single emphasis. If Macaulay did not succeed in portraying humanity in the mass, he made a convincing version of a mass of individual humans. Bards cannot linger too long nor probe too deeply.[92]

But how far did his fulfilment of the needs of his novel-reading public weaken him as a historian? In certain respects, the two forms were less antithetical than is professionally assumed. His one real disaster as a portrait is John Graham of Claverhouse, later Viscount Dundee. Here in his ancestral loyalties he was false to his own sense of obligation to literature. Had he grounded himself initially on the harsh, brutal portrait in Scott's *Old Mortality* with its sense of Claverhouse's grim integrity, loyalty and belief in hierarchical order, he would have at least given a credible performance. His hatred of human cruelty inflamed him beyond reason, and he did not stop to ask himself whether his charges of cruelty to individual Covenanters amounted to the devil-votary he had apparently assumed from his infancy: even in the form he recited them only two of his chosen five cases related to Claverhouse, and in one Claverhouse on Macaulay's showing vainly tried to save the life of his prisoner. The same hatred of cruelty heightened Macaulay's denunciations of George Jeffreys, but here his exaggerations were founded on reality. His last words on Dundee convey his own sense of having broken from his master Scott:

> During the last three months of his life he had approved himself a great warrior and politician; and his name is therefore mentioned with respect by that large class of persons who think that there is no excess of wickedness for which courage and ability do not atone.

The shade of Zachary would have approved; so too would the

shade of Burke in the context of Warren Hastings. The words are highly applicable to the defences of Marlborough later offered by historians of his victories under Queen Anne, notably Macaulay's own grand-nephew George Macaulay Trevelyan. But on Dundee they simply highlight the improbability of Macaulay's narrative. A trigger-happy, sadistic diabolist such as he had described could never have possessed the diplomacy and patience to hold so disparate an army of Highlanders together and lead them to victory at Killiecrankie; a hard-bitten, ruthless, subtle, reflective martinet such as Scott describes could.[93]

Where the demands of the novelist and of the historian part company is on proof. The historical novelist, whatever claims she or he may have to accuracy, is entitled to proceed on the basis of a reasonable supposition. Macaulay himself had stated in 1828 that the historian 'relates no fact ... which is not authenticated by sufficient testimony'. But in his *Lays* he had schooled himself in the novelist's choices. Folk villains are often cowards as well as brutes, and Macaulay's imaginary bards might reasonably be expected to foster the image of the rapist Sextus Tarquinius as a coward: it is part of the childhood hope that the terrifying enemy can easily be put to flight if only one is brave. We might expect the paternal bard in 'Horatius' to make much of this, and it is reasonable for Macaulay to maintain the tradition in 'Lake Regillus'. Sextus is actually reported by Dionysius as dying with the grand berserk courage associated with Richard III at Bosworth, described by Macaulay himself in an early unpublished poem, 'The Battle of Bosworth Field': Macaulay put some lines from his 'Bosworth', slightly altered, into 'Lake Regillus', but not to Sextus' benefit. Similarly, even in his headnote he had silently omitted the tradition recounted by Dionysius that Horatius was so badly disabled by his fight as to be legally unfit for public office, whence the generosity of his public rewards: Macaulay had no desire to anticipate Ernest Hemingway. But he was entitled to make these choices for myths. In the *History* he did so involuntarily but still to his peril. Even so, his difficulties often arose in the early forcing of his hand and conditioning of his mind by influential secondary sources.[94]

Mackintosh's fragment included a particularly deplorable error which Macaulay followed, in assuming that William Penn the Quaker was the 'Mr Penne' involved in traffic with the ladies of

James II's Court as an agent in a money-making venture selling prisoners from Monmouth's revolt as slaves in the West Indies. The man in question was evidently one George Penne: having in all innocence framed William Penn, Macaulay was most unreasonable in fighting off arguments about George Penne as suggested for corrections in later editions. He evidently wavered on the point and might even have ultimately recanted had he lived, but he refused this recantation among the many corrections he made in the last revisions he would live to make. He declared that he had found (very) occasional spellings of William Penn's name as 'Penne'; Mackintosh had said Penne was Penn and so had everyone else; George Penne was a low-class adventurer, and he was involved in petitions as a lottery agent, while William Penn was well connected at Court, the maids of honour had first sought the agency of Sir Francis Warre of Hestercomb, Bart., MP and would be content with 'no ordinary jobber', and had refused the town clerk of Bridgwater; Secretary Sunderland had written dryly and distantly to Penne not because of his recipient's low status but because it was customary, as might be seen by the dry and distant officialese in which the Duke of Wellington's brother had officially written to him; and Oldmixon who had said nothing to the purpose was untrustworthy. Macaulay concluded: 'If it be said that it is incredible that so good a man would have been concerned in so bad an affair, I can only answer that this affair was very far indeed from being the worst in which he was concerned.' Hugh Trevor-Roper correctly states that after writing the original passage 'every incident in which Penn appeared was misinterpreted in order to fit, and to aggravate, the character thus ascribed to him'. But he is unreasonable in his turn in saying that Macaulay hated Penn 'because he hated Quakers'. In the essay on Sir William Temple Macaulay, having evidently missed the slave-agent reference in his first (1835) reading of Mackintosh, had contrasted Penn most favourably to Shaftesbury:

There were in that age some honest men, such as William Penn, who valued toleration so highly that they would willingly have seen it established even by an illegal exertion of the [Royal] prerogative. There were many honest men who dreaded arbitrary power so much that, on account of the alliance between Popery and arbitrary power, they were disposed to grant no toleration to Papists. On both those classes we look with indulgence, though we think both in the wrong. But Shaftesbury belonged to neither class.

It was the slave-trading charge that set Macaulay off: *pace* Trevor-Roper, love was a more powerful emotion than hatred at least for Macaulay, and Zachary was speaking through his son. The mixture of pious sentiment, Court favour and slave traffic summoned up the memory of the forces which had so long blocked Zachary's crusade for reform and sought to blacken his name. In consequence, William Penn's other dealings as an agent between James II and the Baptists, or James II and Magdalen College, Oxford, were rendered on the assumption that Penn was acting for the Court in its attempts to win nonconformist support against Anglicans or infiltrate Roman Catholics into Anglican posts. The truth was that Penn, known as one of the rare Protestants standing in James's favour, was being solicited by less favoured Protestants to negotiate for them. Penn's error lay in putting too much faith in the dazzling advantage of Royal favour, and his most recent students suspect he did not remain entirely unscathed morally, but still he merited the tone of the Temple essay and decidedly not that of the *History*. Macaulay finally compounded his errors by yet another misidentification, this time confusing Penn with the Jacobite agent Nevil Penn or Payne. To unsay all of this would have been not only to tear many passages in the *History* asunder but would have significantly altered the artistic relationship in which the characters stood to one other. This explains much of the obstinacy, and even rudeness, with which Macaulay answered his critics. He was receptive to criticism which simply involved the alteration of single passages. His most persistent opponent, Penn's biographer William Hepworth Dixon, was generous in his acknowledgement of Macaulay's progress on Penn, however, and believed he was reconsidering the whole question in the days before he died.[95]

But it proved to be his nemesis. The Quakers were seriously hurt and various refutations were prepared, among others by the future Liberal Cabinet Minister W.E.Forster, brother-in-law of Matthew Arnold. The last of these attempts in Macaulay's lifetime was the commissioning of a Whig placeman, the lawyer John Paget, now out of a job. Paget produced a long pamphlet on Penn, although the ground of Macaulay's errors and presumed errors had been

pretty thoroughly worked over by Forster and Dixon: it may have
been set on foot by his father-in-law, William Rathbone, one of
the Liverpool philanthropic dynasty of Quaker stock and links. It
was printed by the brothers Blackwood of Edinburgh, whose Tory
journal had been from its foundation locked in vendetta against
the *Edinburgh Review*. The Blackwoods were delighted at the prospect of a champion against the *Edinburgh*'s prize product, and
with the support of their resident academic adviser, the neo-Jacobite
Professor of English at Edinburgh William Edmonstoune Aytoun,
commissioned other attacks from Paget against Macaulay in *Blackwood's Magazine*: on Marlborough (whom Paget defended by stating that the Treasurer Sidney Godolphin was also giving treasonable
information on troop movements to James and Louis), on the Highlands (complaining about Macaulay's paucity of source-material,
thus proving – unwittingly – how much the account owed to family
traditions and Sir Walter Scott), on Glencoe (insisting that Macaulay
had blackened the Master of Stair in order to exculpate William
III), and on Dundee (with justice, but owing much to previous critiques from Aytoun and Mark Napier). Paget paraded them in a
volume entitled *The New Examen* as soon as the decencies and
John Blackwood permitted after Macaulay's death, of which Paget
was anxious to take full marketing advantage. He was savaged at
considerable length in the *Edinburgh* (October 1861), but showed
that the parasite growth could imitate its prey by proving more
obdurate even than Macaulay in his refusal to answer the refutations
produced there by the Lord Advocate, Sir James Moncreiff. The
book was brought out again in 1874 as part of Paget's *Paradoxes
and Puzzles*. Leslie Stephen adopted its arguments in the DNB.
T.F.Henderson (a collaborator of the High Tory journalist W.E.
Henley) in the only annotated edition Macaulay's *History* ever
obtained, accepted almost all Paget's emendations, being apparently
unaware of Moncreiff's wounding rejoinder which had faulted him
badly on Marlborough and Glencoe. And in 1934 Winston Churchill brought out Paget once more, with copious lamentation at
its 'having fallen stillborn from the press' in 1862 (as Trevor-Roper
puts it, loyally following Churchill's ignorance). The general effect
was to frighten academics away from Macaulay, or at least to create
an *a priori* assumption that he was a hopelessly partisan trickster
who falsified his evidence. Paget's charges were accepted also by
Sir Charles Firth in his *A Commentary on Macaulay's History of*

England (another posthumous fragment), although otherwise Firth made a wise presentation of the state of scholarship when Macaulay wrote. In general, Paget was taken for an honest Whig, as against the dishonest Whig Macaulay.[96]

The great reappraisal of Macaulay's work in recent years by Professors John Clive, Thomas Pinney, Joseph Hamburger, and others has brought scholars back to the real ideological impulses and ethics that governed Macaulay. Dr Hamburger, in particular, has doubted whether it is reasonable to think of Macaulay as a Whig historian at all. Significantly the late Sir Herbert Butterfield, who defined the Whig interpretation of history in 1931 as exalting Protestantism, progress and a supposed Whig tradition in defence of the constitution, firmly listed Macaulay's second essay on the elder Pitt among the non-Whig interpretations of the supposed constitutional crisis at the accession of George III; but his minute examination of its historiography highlighted Macaulay's nephew and biographer George Otto Trevelyan as the author of an extreme Whig view in his *The Early History of Charles James Fox*. The contrast is telling. Trevelyan's *The Life and Letters of Lord Macaulay* (1875) made much of its subject's Whiggism, and argued for his party spirit in historical writing. It would have been to Trevelyan's political advantage to assert such ideological orthodoxy in his most eminent relative: it gave himself a tradition of political reliability. The biography became extremely popular and supplied the waiting critics from Stephen to Gladstone with further evidence of Macaulay's partisanship. Trevelyan's ruthless but silent dovetailing and cutting of Macaulay's letters and journal heightened the effect he sought, and narrowed the man he described. The publication of the *Letters* in the 1970s and the opening of the journal to students have produced a different and much more complex figure.[97]

Macaulay's *History* was concerned with revolution, but with something much more than 1688 and its immediate sequel. The late Raymond Williams, one of the finest historians of literature in our time, remarked in his *The Long Revolution* (1961), 'where we read Macaulay, we read perhaps with less interest, not because his ability seems less, but because his way of thinking seems increasingly irrelevant'. But the failure of the left in Britain today does not detract from the value of Williams's own constructive criticism and evangelical vigour. Similarly the passing of the immediate limitations on Macaulay's contemporary horizon does not detract from the value of reading him. In the circumstances Williams's title becomes ironic as well as instructive. Macaulay's *History* moves its readers, in whatever era they may read it, to the contemplation of one phase of a long revolution, and was intended to play a major part in another phase, with which Williams's own narrative was intimately concerned. Macaulay was part of the Age of the Democratic Revolution, which R.R.Palmer saw as spanning the later eighteenth century but with whose long-term implications Macaulay and his contemporaries were deeply engaged. The real purpose of the *History* was to absorb his readers in the past in its totality, above all in its culture. In doing so Macaulay saw himself as devising the means by which the future would show its title to rule. As Dr Hamburger has argued, the *History*'s purpose was in part to show through such figures as Halifax how any society must guard itself from destruction by the victory of a single interest or passion, that ideology must meet ideology in full exchange, and that the absolute victory of any representative political force would be destructive of the harmony of society. Macaulay's pioneering account of the reign of William III warned time and again of the danger of excess, and towards the end of the reign he saw signs of a tendency to permanent revolution in the violence of the xenophobia against William's Dutch friends. Macaulay's own vehemence might seem reminiscent of the vehemence of Edmund Burke, which he deplored but sought to understand. He was Burke's disciple in believing that any society could only preserve itself by cultivating its sense of the past, and by recognizing the advantages it had won by the study of the conflicts and circumstances that had won them. He was anxious to teach principles of honour, integrity, decency, courage and the search for cultural discovery at all levels. If his presentation of character was intended to entertain, it was also intended to instruct and – for he wrote in grief and loss and defeat – to console. He believed in freedom; he believed that without knowledge of its origin it was meaningless and self-destructive. His inherited detestation of slavery made him the evangelist against servility of any kind, and it was this which charged so much of his writing against monarchical power and Court influence. His first chapter preached the good fortune of accident, declaring that the absence of effective kingship prevented permanent national subordination to the mystification of kingship. But while in an ideal sense he held that the King must die, he regarded the martyrdom of Charles I as productive of the renewal of mystification. It is this that accounts for his almost wilful irrationality in the portrait of James II. He did not, after all, retreat from the tradition of republicanism; he offered another target for demystification without the folly of Royal reconsecration by blood sacrifice. In lampooning and traducing James he was playing out the Spirit's advice in Milton's *Comus*:

> the rod reversed,
> And backward mutters of dissevering power....

Charles's execution had simply inaugurated the rule of shadow in place of substance: the inauguration of vigilante government judging by outward signs of conformity prevented the inauguration of freedom of communications, and by imposing artificial censorship simply invited hypocrisy and its eventual replacement by cynicism. What followed James II was no new Paradise in Macaulay's description, nor did Macaulay relax his hatred of unprincipled politics, but he proclaimed what was gained in the snapping of individual curbs on human liberty.[98]

His *History* by bringing to life an epoch, even with heightened and sometimes distorted foci, won its American audience as much as anything by telling the mid-nineteenth-century Americans what their ancestors had meant in 1776 when they revolted in the name of those liberties and the circumstances of their acquisition. The Age of the Democratic Revolution itself was initially set on foot because of certain loose ideas about the meaning of 1688, ideas which became even looser as they were transported to France. Macaulay was trying to show what had been the reality invoked in those images. He was apprehensive about the future of what they produced in America and in France, though he was ready to defend the attempt to invoke them, if not – in the most literal sense in France – the execution which followed the invocation. He presented the Revolution's legislative achievements, and examined their weaknesses for future times, with the care of a draughtsman as well as of a student of the working out of ideological confrontation. His admiration for the achievement into which the English had entered partly by design and partly by accident did not lead him to assume it could be crudely duplicated in other countries by ideological conviction on the part of conscientious imitators: Washington, apparently the least intellectual of the American leaders and the most responsive to the immediate dictates of his local situation, received his highest praise.

The argument that has been raised against his judgments, that they were formed early and implacably adhered to, has only a relative justification. There were, indeed, different stages of evolution in portions of his judgment. If he condemned Marlborough when he was twenty-eight, he seems only to have worked out what he thought Marlborough was really trying to do in his forties or early fifties. If he condemned Dundee almost in his cradle, his careful examination of the ground of his last campaign in the years he was writing brought home to him what formidable obstacles Dundee had encountered, how he overcame them, and how effectively he rose from them. Macaulay's close scrutiny of his sources meant that, in the process of writing, other old targets of criticism began to gain his respect, among them the Tory leader Thomas Osborne, Earl of Danby, whom he had consigned to his own Inferno in the Temple essay along with Marlborough and Dundee. But in another sense the antiquity of some of his impressions gave an extraordinary freshness to his writing. He held a great deal of the eagerness of a boy in his enthusiasm and excitement. The basis for *The Lays of Ancient Rome* lay in highly esoteric classical scholarship and comparative analysis of folk cultures headed by the Anglo-Scottish 'borderers'. But the lays themselves owed much to the hold he retained on his youth, and the *History* captured some of the same bardic involvement in the battles, where James and Louis drew some of his creative involvement with Tarquin and Lars Porsena. 'What a grand writer for the young Macaulay is' wrote the seventy-eight-year-old George Lyttelton to his former pupil Rupert Hart-Davis, 'so lucid and emphatic.' Macaulay's rejuvenative effect on his audience owed much to his finding within his work his own mental rejuvenation, so that for a time he could blot out the cruel present and be once more a brother telling stories to little sisters. And in the end the fragments the surviving sister would put together said their final word, not in the great sounding tones of the bard, but with the gentle lyricism and love he hid from the world. It was on the death of his hero William. From his youth he had been deeply grateful to William. As his student essay on him had pointed out, William could so easily have subjected the country he invaded to the humiliation of vindictive purges, to the threat of a further foreign tyranny, to another phase of social conflict and civic strife.

The *History* acknowledged that William's obsession with defeating Louis XIV had subordinated all things, including, as Sir James Moncreiff pointed out, the Highlanders of Glencoe, to his insistence on getting his army back in the field. But William had allowed the domestic arrangements in Britain to be worked out with as little interference as his European aims would permit; his very taciturnity had played its part in the demonarchization of Britain; with so much power apparently within his grasp he had contented himself with what was sensible, as Washington was to do. So the *History* became in its way an ode of gratitude to the alien and lonely figure who was so friendless in his own time, from a man who like William would identify himself with the enduring constitutional settlement of a country of which in person he could never be absolutely representative. And thus in the last words of his *History* Macaulay reached his softest and sweetest melody in the fragment in which he recorded William's death, written as he longed for his own:

> It was now between seven and eight in the morning. He closed his eyes, and gasped for breath. The bishops knelt down and read the commendatory prayer. When it ended William was no more.
>
> When his remains were laid out, it was found that he wore next to his skin a small piece of black silk riband. The lords in waiting ordered it to be taken off. It contained a gold ring and a lock of the hair of Mary.[99]

Notes

As editions of Macaulay's *History* and *Critical and Historical Essays* are very numerous, I have taken the unusual step of citing references by opening of paragraphs in the *Essays* and *Speeches*, and section-titles within the chapters of the *History*. The purpose is to place the quotations within easy reach of every reader instead of only those with recourse to my choice of edition.

1. Thomas Pinney, ed., *The Letters of Thomas Babington Macaulay* I (1974), xii–xxix. John Clive, *Macaulay: The Shaping of the Historian* (1973), 3–22.
2. Capt. F. W. L. Thomas, 'Traditions of the Macaulays of Lewis', *Proceedings of the Society of Antiquaries of Scotland*, XIV (new ser. II), 100th session 1879–80, 363–430. George Otto Trevelyan, *The Life and Letters of Lord Macaulay* (1876), ch. I, and the opening pages of [Margaret ('Baba') Holland (*née* Trevelyan)] Viscountess Knutsford, *Life and Letters of Zachary Macaulay* (1900) indicate surviving family traditions. Thomas Babington Macaulay, *The History of England from the Accession of James the Second* (1849), ch. I ('His Execution'), ch. 4 ('The King detained near Sheerness', 'The Lords order him to be set at Liberty; William's embarrassment'). *The Lyon in Mourning*, I, 204.
3. James Boswell, *Journal of a Tour to the Hebrides with Samuel Johnson in 1773*, ed. Frederick A. Pottle and Charles H. Bennett (1963): 25 October 1773 (at 353–7). Macaulay, 'Boswell's Life of Johnson', and *Critical and Historical Essays Contributed to the Edinburgh Review* ('We are not sure...').
4. *Letters*, I, xxi–xxv. Knutsford, *Zachary Macaulay*.
5. *Ibid.* Christopher Fyfe, *A History of Sierra Leone* (1962) and *Sierra Leone Inheritance* (1964).
6. The best answer to Macaulay on Dundee may be found in G. K. Chesterton, 'The Dagger with Wings' (*The Incredulity of*

Father Brown, ch. 8 (followed by a passage in agreement with his view of the Master of Stair)). William Edmonstoune Aytoun, *Lays of the Scottish Cavaliers*, included a refutatory appendix in his second and subsequent editions (1849, etc.) and because his own work pursued the same readership as Macaulay's *Lays of Ancient Rome* he had logic as well as justification – and many imitators in his turn.

7. Trevelyan, *Macaulay*, ch. 1, and Knutsford, *Zachary Macaulay*, with the usual *caveats* on letters quoted. Clive, *Macaulay*, chs. 1–3 (which assumes more father–son hostility). Zachary Macaulay to Macaulay, 12 November 1811 (quoted Knutsford, 291–2) and 25 February 1813 (*Letters*, I, 19n.). Macaulay to Zachary, 1 June 1811, 8 May 1813, 5 February 1819 (*ibid.*, 7, 30, 118–21). Macaulay to his sister Selina, 25 October 1813 (*ibid.*, 38). Macaulay to his mother, 17 April 1815 (*ibid.*, 60–1). Zachary to his wife, 7 June 1823 (*ibid.*, 187n., and see Macaulay to Zachary, 7 ? June, 187–9). Charles Knight, *Passages of a Working Life*, I (1864), 304–34. Robert Montgomery, *The Age Reviewed* (quoted *Letters*, I, 267n., and see *ibid.*, V, 33, 103, 387–88 ; VI, 269). Boswell, *Life of Johnson*, 23 September 1777. Macaulay, 'Boswell's Life of Johnson', ('Of the talents which ordinarily raise men ...').

8. Macaulay, 'Warren Hastings' ('Of all his errors the most serious ...', 'The zeal of Burke was still fiercer ...', 'That good and great man, the late William Wilberforce ...'). Arthur Roberts, ed., *Letters of Hannah More to Zachary Macaulay* (1860).

9. Clive, *Macaulay*, 72 (a passage Peter Gay, *Style in History* (1975) misinterprets as conveying paternal sadism), and ch. 10, a definitive treatment of Macaulay's relations with Hannah and Margaret. Margaret Macaulay, *Recollections by a Sister of T.B.Macaulay*, in [J.B.Macaulay,] *Memoirs of the Clan 'Aulay'* (1881) : introductory paragraphs. The unfinished MS was a conscious effort at Boswellism.

10. Clive, *Macaulay*, 47, and ch. 3 in general. Knight, *Passages*, I, chs. 9–10. *Letters*, I, Biographical Chronology (Professor Pinney's chronologies commencing each volume of the *Letters* have been invaluable to me in this sketch of Macaulay's life), and excellent biographical notes, on first main reference to individuals. Tristram Merton [Macaulay], 'Scenes from *Athenian Revels* : a Drama', *Knight's Quarterly Magazine*, II (January

1824), 21, 23.

11. *Knight's*, II (January 1824), 33–5 : Merton [Macaulay], 'Songs of the Huguenots'. *Ibid.* (April 1824), 321–5 : 'Songs of the Civil War'.

12. Joseph Hamburger, *Macaulay and the Whig Tradition* (1976) is indispensable for the student who wishes to pursue the question. I have slight differences from him on minor points.

13. Merton [Macaulay], 'Some account of the Law-Suit between the Parishes of St Dennis and St George in the Water. Part I', *Knight's*, II (April 1824), 404–11 (no second part published : the first part breaks off with the marriage of 'Solicitor Nap' to the daughter of 'Lord Caesar Germain', i.e. Napoleon's marriage to the Archduchess Marie Louise of Austria in 1810). 'A Conversation between Mr Abraham Cowley and Mr John Milton, touching the great Civil War', *Knight's*, III (August 1824), 17–33 (*Knight's* was by now dropping its policy of (pseudonymous) signature for articles but exceptionally this is still 'T.M.' on its conclusion). Edmund Wilson, *Patriotic Gore : Studies in the Literature of the American Civil War* (1962), 91–7.

14. 'WALKER, William Sidney (1795–1846)', *Dictionary of National Biography*. (Walker died destitute : Macaulay sent at least £40 to help his sister's financial need between 1856 and 1859. *Letters*, VI, 34n.) The Rev. John Moultrie (1799–1874), another of Macaulay's friends writing for *Knight's*, edited Walker's *Poetry and Remains* (1852) with a memoir noticing Walker's work on the Milton MS. Macaulay's discovery by the *Edinburgh* is reviewed comprehensively by Pinney (*Letters*, I, 203n.), noticing in passing that *Blackwood's* had been advised to try to recruit him in May 1824 ; the family firm's subsequent vendetta against him (see Chapter 4) may have owed something to bitterness at the thought of the one that got away.

15. As Pinney notes, 'E.E.Kellett, a good judge, has said that, with the possible exception of Ruskin, [Macaulay] is the Victorian writer "whose pages show the closest acquaintance with our Bible" (*London Quarterly Review*, 148 [1927], 203)' (*Letters*, II, 22n.). The entire Kellett essay is most helpful, as is anything else he has written on Macaulay or alluding to him.

16. Macaulay's change of the *Edinburgh*'s tune on Wordsworth was maliciously noted in a remarkable American analysis of the *Edinburgh* and its rivals ('The British Critics', *North*

American Review, LXI (October 1845), 471), though it inaccurately ascribed it to a change in public opinion : the passage
occurs in Macaulay's essay on Moore's *Life of Byron* (*Edinburgh*, June 1831) ('It was in description and meditation that
Byron excelled...'). The 'Milton' passages begin 'We must con-
clude...' and 'Therefore it is that we decidedly approve of the
conduct of Milton....'

17. So begins the paragraph of 'Milton' in question.

18. 'The London University' (*Edinburgh*, February 1826) ; 'The
Present Administration' (*Edinburgh*, June 1827). On the SDUK,
Pinney as almost always anticipates virtually every want of his
readers : *Letters*, I, 322–3 (appendix, quoting Ellis to Brougham, 14 September 1828). Macaulay's maiden speech, on Jewish Disabilities, 5 April 1830, of which a version appears in
Hansard, 2nd ser., XXIII, 1308–14, must be distinguished from
his speech on the same subject on 17 April 1833, which he
reprinted in his *Speeches* (1854 [1853]), as well as from his
Edinburgh essay (January 1831) included by him in *Critical
and Historical Essays*.

19. 'This work has greatly disappointed us....'

20. The Leeds diarist, a shopkeeper, is quoted by Clive, *Macaulay*,
222, and in its entirety his ch. 8 ('Holland House and Leeds')
is most useful. Georgiana Devonshire and Grey make their
appearances in 'Hastings' following 'The place was worthy of
such a trial...' and 'But neither the culprit nor his advocates
attracted so much notice as the accusers...' and each of them
closes the respective paragraphs.

21. Macaulay to Ellis, 30 March 1831, *Letters*, II, 10–11. Macaulay's 'Political Georgics' appeared in *The Times* 18 March 1828
and was reprinted by Ellis in his edition of *The Miscellaneous
Writings of Lord Macaulay* (1861), Herries's name having
initial only. Macaulay to his sister Hannah, 29 June and 1 July
1831, discuss the work and reprint a fuller text of it (*Letters*,
II, 56–62).

22. Macaulay to his sisters Hannah and Margaret, 8 June 1832
(*Letters*, II, 124). A clash with Lansdowne on Macaulay's belief
in resisting a rejection of Reform in the Lords by the creation
of new peers is described to Hannah, 13 September 1831 (*ibid.*,
II, 100).

23. 'Milton' ('The book itself will not add much to the fame of

Milton...'). The line on Quintilian is in Milton's Sonnet XI. The second essay on the elder Pitt, reprinted in editions of *Critical and Historical Essays* subsequent to its *Edinburgh* publication, was titled 'The Earl of Chatham' and the section quoted is from the paragraph beginning 'This was not all. The spirit of party...'.

24. 'The destinies of our Indian empire are covered with thick darkness...' (*Speeches*: here and elsewhere I have used only his own compilation). Pinney's persuasive conjecture on Macaulay's reading of Mill is based on Macaulay to his sisters Hannah and Margaret, 10 June 1832 (*Letters*, II, 129 and n.). Macaulay to Zachary, 12 October 1836 (*Letters*, III, 193). See also Eric Stokes, *The English Utilitarians and India* (1959), and Clive, *Macaulay*, chs. 11–14. For Macaulay on Robinson Crusoe, see his essay on Dryden ('We do not mean to say that the contemporaries of Dante...') reprinted by Ellis in *Miscellaneous Writings*: it does not discuss Friday's education but it says everything about the book's hold on Macaulay. For Macaulay on Bentinck, see *Letters*, III, 31n.

25. On Homer's illiteracy, 'Sir James Mackintosh's History of the Revolution' ('This gentleman can never want matter for pride, if he finds it so easily...').

26. Trevelyan's ascription of Virginia's origin to Baba is in his *Macaulay*, ch. IX, where he discusses the reception of the *Lays*. The Lichfield visit was on 7–8 April 1849 (Journal, I, 562–9).

27. Macaulay to Ellis, 30 December 1835 (*Letters*, III, 158).

28. 'Lord Bacon' (*Edinburgh*, July 1837): 'We are by no means without sympathy for Mr Montagu even in what we consider as his weakness....'

29. Macaulay to his sister Hannah, 20 March 1839 (*Letters*, III, 280).

30. Macaulay to 'My dear Charley', 20 June 1842, 27 July 1843 (*Letters*, III, 39, 134). Macaulay to Ellis, 17 April 1847 (*ibid.*, 334 and n., where Pinney sadly records 'He died, like his mother, of scarlet fever').

31. As to 'Sir William Temple', so begins the paragraph in question. In 'Gladstone on Church and State' (*Edinburgh*, April 1839): 'Do we make this diversity a topic of reproach to the Church of England?'

32. I base myself on a reading of his journal for these months.

It is only fair to say that Professor Jane Millgate's admirable *Macaulay* (1973) finds the same source more anti-Catholic than I do.

33. I have discussed the poem in the context of *The Flying Dutchman* in 'Those in Peril – and the Sea', *Scottish Opera Yearbook 1986/1987*, 41–8.

34. 'War with China' (*Speeches* : 'I have now, Sir, gone through the four heads of the charge...'). Macaulay to Ebrington, 6 January (and see also 12 January) 1841 (*Letters*, III, 360–1 and 362). Macaulay to his sister (probably Frances), early October 1839 (*Letters*, III, 304) : the letter survives only in a fragment printed in Trevelyan, leaving the suspicion that excised portions may have been more irreverent still.

35. Macaulay to Napier, 20 July 1838 (*Letters*, III, 252). It is famous that Macaulay visited battlefields, but less stressed that he pursued local enquiries about folk-memory. At Sedgemoor he noted that time had altered the battlefield far more than the folk-memory (*History*, ch. 5 : 'the Royal Army encamps at Sedgemoor', 'Battle of Sedgemoor').

36. 'The State of Ireland' (*Speeches* : 'But you were incorrigible...').

37. 'The People's Charter' (*Speeches* : 'The Chartists demand annual parliaments...' ; 'I am far from wishing to throw any blame...' ; and for the last two extracts 'But it is said, You must not attach so much importance...').

38. 'Maynooth' (*Speeches* : 'In such terms I feel it to be my duty...' ; 'But, Sir, am I, because I think thus...'). Macaulay to the Electors of Edinburgh, 2 August 1847 (*Letters*, IV, 345). John Robinson, *The Macaulay Election (of 1846) ; or, the Designs of the Ministry.... The Macaulay Rejection (of 1847)* (1847).

39. Macaulay to his sister Frances, 6 August 1847 (and see also Macaulay to Adam Black (?), 11 August 1847 (*Letters*, IV, 348(–9)).

40. Sir Charles Firth, *A Commentary on Macaulay's History of England* (1938), ch. 4 : 'Macaulay's Use of Authorities'. The volume was posthumously published, being edited by Godfrey Davies, and like its subject is unfinished.

41. Macaulay to Andrew Rutherfurd, 16 November 1848 (*Letters*, IV, 380 and n.). 'Inaugural Address as Lord Rector, University of Glasgow' (*Speeches* : 'At this conjuncture, a conjuncture of unrivalled interest in the history of letters...').

42. *Ibid*. : 'A fifth secular period is about to commence ...' ; 'I trust, therefore, that, when a hundred years more have run out ...'.

43. Macaulay to Lady Theresa Lewis, 28 March 1849 (*Letters*, v, 40–1). Journal, III, 16a.

44. 'The day before yesterday I had a regular fainting fit, and lay quite insensible. I wish that I had continued to lie so. For if death be no more – Up I got however ; and the Doctors agree that the circumstance is altogether unimportant' (Macaulay to Ellis, 25 December 1859, *Letters*, VI, 261). Ellis, Hannah and Charles Trevelyan were listed in his will (dated 28 October 1858) as his executors. Baba received £10,000, her brother George and sister Alice £5,000 each, his surviving brothers John and Charles £5,000 each, his sister Frances £2,000, his late brother Henry's two sons £1,000 each, Ellis £1,000 and his choice of 100 volumes of printed books, Hannah the residue (over £40,000) as well as the rest of the library, furniture and real estate. Ellis proved the will on 12 January 1860 (*The Times*, 23 January 1860). Hannah would have obtained large sums from subsequent royalties, but she nonetheless sold much of the library soon afterwards. That the personal estate was not greater may be put down to Macaulay's many private acts of generosity.

45. *Letters*, v, 79n., and IV, 44n. Matthew Arnold, *On Translating Homer : Last Words* (1862), reprinted in R.H.Super, ed., *The Complete Prose Writings of Matthew Arnold*, I, 211, and see also 131 ('one continual falsetto, like the pinchbeck *Roman Ballads* of Lord Macaulay').

46. Leslie Stephen, *Hours in a Library*, 3rd ser. (1879), 315, 303, 305–6. Reprinted from the *Cornhill*, and, like so much more belittling comment from men of letters of this time, arising from publication of G.O.Trevelyan, *Macaulay*, whose portrait of Macaulay as Whig is basic to Stephen's thesis : 'Whiggism seemed to him to provide a satisfactory solution for all political problems.... Macaulay thus early became a thorough-going Whig. Whiggism seemed to him the *ne plus ultra* of progress.... Macaulay is the genuine representative of the pure Whig type.... Here again Macaulay is a true Whig.... Macaulay was not only a typical Whig, but the prophet of Whiggism to his generation' (*ibid.*, 286, 288, 293, 299, 306).

47. Macaulay to James Henry Leigh Hunt, 19 November 1844 (*Letters*, IV, 223).
48. Lafcadio Hearn, 'The Value of Supernatural in Fiction', a lecture delivered when Hearn was Professor of English Literature in the University of Tokyo, 1896–1902 in his *Interpretations of Literature*, ed. John Erskine (1916) II, 92–3.
49. Macaulay to Selina Mills Macaulay, 26 October 1814 (*Letters*, I, 53). 'History' (Ellis, ed., *Miscellaneous Writings*) : 'Livy had some faults in common with these writers....' J.W.Burrow, *A Liberal Descent : Victorian Historians and the English Past* (1981) has been a most valuable stimulus to my ideas on Macaulay's use of history as civic preparation, but I cannot share his view that this passage constitutes a *defence* of Livy (p. 59), even if as he puts it 'Livy was a Whig'. In any case Dr Burrow wisely and constructively retreats from his stress on Macaulay's Whiggism in his next chapter.
50. Macaulay to his sister Hannah, 14 October 1833, 15 ? November 1833 (*Letters*, II, 317, 336–7). Macaulay's attitude to family custody of ancestral papers and reputations may be seen in 'Lord Spencer has invited me to rummage his family papers ; a great proof of liberality when it is considered that he is the lineal descendant of Sunderland and Marlborough. In general it is ludicrous to see how sore people are at seeing the truth told about their ancestors' (Macaulay to his sister Frances, 19 December 1849, *Letters*, V, 84), an amusing if unconscious prophecy of the response his *History* induced in their later descendant Winston Churchill. Trevelyan, *Macaulay*, Appendix, includes the lengthy note Macaulay appended to Livy, Book XXVII, on the Metaurus.
51. Chesterton, *Victorian Age in Literature* (1913), 32. 'Ranke's History of the Popes' : 'Then, again, all the great enigmas which perplex the natural theologian are the same in all ages....' 'Dryden' : so begin the paragraphs in question.
52. *History* : ch. 13, 'State of the Highlands' (twice) ; ch. 18, 'Glencoe' ; ch. 13, 'Lochiel' and 'Military Character of the Highlanders'.
53. Arnold also agreed with Macaulay's hostility to Dr Johnson's attack on 'The Bard'.
54. *History* : ch. 13, 'the Highland Army Reinforced', 'State of the Highlands'.

55. Chesterton, *The Victorian Age in Literature*, 31.
56. Pinney (*Letters*, VI, 301) dates 'Epitaph on a Jacobite' 8 May
    1847. Ellis (*Miscellaneous Writings*) inaccurately gives 1845.
    Macaulay is supposed to have written the poem during a com-
    mittee meeting and given it across the table to his friend Mahon.
57. Macaulay to Leigh Hunt, 27 March 1841, to Macvey Napier,
    26 April 1841 (*Letters*, III, 369, 371). Southey's death was
    then believed imminent, but when he died in 1843 the Laur-
    eateship was given to Wordsworth. Aytoun and his collaborator
    Theodore Martin, future biographer of Victoria's Prince Con-
    sort Albert, in their *The Book of Ballads* (1847), signed 'Bon
    Gaultier' and published by Blackwood, included a parody of
    'Ivry' ('The Royal Banquet') in which Macaulay seeks the Laur-
    eateship for himself.
58. *Speeches* : 'Repeal of the Union with Ireland', 6 February 1833.
    'I would act towards Ireland on the same principles on which
    I acted towards England....' *History* : ch. 17 'State of Ireland
    after the War'.
59. W. W. Robson, 'Tennyson and Victorian Balladry', to be pub-
    lished in a volume of essays on Tennyson, ed. Philip Collins
    (1989).
60. Arnold's essay on Joseph Joubert (*National Review* (January
    1864)), declared Macaulay to be 'the great apostle of the Philis-
    tines' (Arnold, *Prose Writings*, ed. Super, III, 210). Stephen
    took it from there.
61. 'Mr Robert Montgomery's Poems' : 'Mr Robert Montgomery
    is fond of personification....'
62. 'Mr Robert Montgomery's Poems' : so begins the paragraph
    in question. 'Some Account of the Law-Suit between the Par-
    ishes of St Dennis and St George in the Water', *Knight's*, II
    (April 1824), 408. Hazlitt preceded Macaulay in the attempt
    to reclaim Burke from the right (Michael Foot, *The Politics
    of Paradise : A Vindication of Byron* (1988), 20–3), and was
    apparently an important literary influence on Macaulay's
    youthful progress to the left.
63. 'Barère' (Ellis, ed., *Miscellaneous Writings*) : 'It would be
    grossly unjust, we acknowledge, to try a man situated as Barère
    was by a severe standard....'
64. 'Warren Hastings' (*Edinburgh*, October 1841) : 'If it were

worth while to examine this performance in detail...'. At Gleig's earnest request Macaulay dropped this paragraph from new editions of his essays (Macaulay to Gleig, 22 June 1851, *Letters*, v, 169 and n.), but it continued to appear in ordinary reprints of *Critical and Historical Essays* until in 1903 F.C.Montague excised it from his annotated text. It is restored in sensible anthologies (Gleig having died in 1888), such as G.M.Young, ed., *Macaulay: Prose and Poetry* (1952) in Rupert Hart-Davis's Reynard Library. 'Frederic the Great' (*Edinburgh*, April 1842): 'At this moment he was assailed by a new enemy....' The 'schooner of pirates' looks like the inspiration for the song 'The Pirate King' in W.S.Gilbert and Arthur Sullivan, *The Pirates of Penzance*.

65. Macaulay to Napier, 26 June 1838 (*Letters*, III, 245). 'Diary and Letters of Madame D'Arblay': 'Miss Burney did for the English novel what Jeremy Collier did for the English drama; and she did it in a better way....'

66. Macaulay to Napier, 18 April 1842 (*Letters*, IV, 27–8). The fashion in cant has sufficiently changed for it to be necessary to say a 'bore' to Macaulay was a tedious person, not an annoying occurrence, and an 'awkward squad' was an ill-regulated military body, not a factious group of civilians. He at least had logic on his side.

67. 'Burleigh and His Times': so begins the paragraph in question. 'Milton': 'That from which the public character of Milton derives its great and peculiar splendour...'. Macaulay to Napier, 24 June 1842 (*Letters*, IV, 40–1).

68. 'Machiavelli': so begins the paragraph in question.

69. I have not discussed this work, as Macaulay never finished nor revised it. It was lost for many decades and the surviving fragment was edited by Professor Joseph Hamburger under the title *Napoleon and the Restoration of the Bourbons* (1977). Our thanks are due to him, but its author might reasonably feel it should have no place in a historian's assessment of the historical writing he published.

70. 'Lord Nugent's Memorials of Hampden': 'We have read this book with great pleasure....' 'Gladstone on Church and State': 'The author of this volume is a young man of unblemished character....'

71. 'Burleigh and his Times': 'That which is, as we have said, the

great stain on the character of Burleigh...'. 'Hallam's Constitutional History' : 'England has no such names to show...' (twice). Montague, ed., *Critical and Historical Essays Contributed to the Edinburgh Review by Lord Macaulay* (1903), I, 127n. 'Hallam's Constitutional History' : 'Such was the theory of that thorough reform in the state which Strafford meditated....'

72. 'Hallam's Constitutional History' : 'The time at which Charles took this step...' ; 'The Constitution of England was only one of a large family....'

73. *Ibid.* : so begins the first paragraph in question ; 'But for the weakness of that foolish Ishbosheth, the opinions which we have been expressing would, we believe, now have formed the orthodox creed of good Englishmen....'

74. *Ibid.* : so begins the first paragraph in question ; 'But the reproach was not confined to the Church....' 'Sir William Temple' : 'Yet Temple is not a man to our taste....'

75. 'Hallam's Constitutional History' : so begins the paragraph in question. John Kenyon, *The History Men : The Historical Profession in England since the Renaissance* (1983), 79. *History* : ch. 10, 'Peculiar Character of the English Revolution'.

76. 'Sir James Mackintosh's History of the Revolution' : so begins the first paragraph in question ; 'But the very considerations which lead us to look forward...' ; 'This gentleman can never want matter for pride....' The editor whose identity Macaulay did not know was an Irish Catholic barrister and journalist, William Bayley Wallace (1793 ?–1839), who challenged both Napier and Macaulay to duels (*Letters*, III, 107n.).

77. 'Hallam's Constitutional History' : 'In the political as in the natural body...'. 'Lord Nugent's Memorials of Hampden' : 'He had indeed left none his like behind him....' For Carlyle's judgment of Macaulay, see *Letters*, II, 113.

78. 'Lord Nugent's Memorials of Hampden' : 'The Scots advanced into England to meet him....' 'Sir James Mackintosh's History of the Revolution' : so begins the paragraph in question, of which the second extract also forms part.

79. Kenyon, *History Men*, 80. Hamburger, *Macaulay and the Whig Tradition*, is a wiser guide, although Kenyon, while careless, is stimulating, and his *Stuart England* (1978, 1985) has been extremely helpful to me. Macaulay to Ellis, 30 December 1835

(*Letters*, III, 158–9). Macaulay to Mahon, 31 December 1836 (*ibid.*, 206).

80. 'Ranke's History of the Popes' : so begins the paragraph in question.

81. 'Leigh Hunt's Comic Dramatists of the Restoration' : 'The plays to which he now acts as introducer...' (twice) ; 'On the contrary, during the forty years which followed the Restoration...' ; 'But we should be justly chargeable with gross inconsistency...' ; 'But, when all deductions have been made...'. Chesterton, *Victorian Age in Literature*, 35.

82. Macaulay to Napier, 1 December 1841 (*Letters*, IV, 17). 'Hallam's Constitutional History' : 'Where such was the political morality of the noble and the wealthy...'. 'Lord Clive' : 'We should not think it necessary to offer any remarks for the purpose of directing the judgment of our readers....' 'Frederic the Great' : 'Had the Silesian question been merely a question between Frederic and Maria Theresa...'.

83. *Letters*, V, 53n., quoting journal on Charles Russell. Macaulay to Lord John Russell, 3 January 1849 (*ibid.*, 6–7). Macaulay to Mahon, 31 December 1836 (*Letters*, III, 206). 'Sir William Temple' : 'We cannot help adding, though we are extremely unwilling to quarrel with Mr Courtenay about politics...'. David Hume, *The History of England ; from the Invasion of Julius Caesar to the Revolution in 1688* (new edition, 1822), VIII, 308.

84. Macaulay to Napier, 5 November 1841 (*Letters*, IV, 15). 'Diary and Letters of Madame D'Arblay' : 'Shakspeare has had neither equal nor second....'

85. Macaulay to Ellis, 9 March 1850 (*Letters*, V, 99).

86. 'History' (Ellis, ed., *Miscellaneous Writings*) : so begin the paragraphs in question. Ellis to Brougham, 14 September 1828 (*Letters*, I, 322). It is interesting that Ellis at this stage knew his future friend so little that he wrote of him as 'Macauley'. They had met in March 1826 when Ellis found him 'a very amusing person – somewhat boyish in manner, but very original' (*Letters*, I, 218). Ellis was four years older, which was probably significant.

87. *History* : ch. 11, 'Unpopularity of William'.

88. 'Boswell's Life of Johnson' : 'The Life of Johnson is assuredly a great, a very great work....' 'History' : 'Let us suppose that

Lord Clarendon...'. 'JOHNSON, Samuel' (Ellis, ed., *Miscellaneous Writings*) : 'Since his death the popularity of his works...'. *History* : ch. 1, 'Introduction'. 'History' : 'In the works of such writers as these...'. *History* : ch. 19, 'Distress in England'.

89. Clive, 'Macaulay's Historical Imagination', *A Review of English Literature*, I (October 1960), 28. (The entire number, edited by A.Norman Jeffares, contains several important essays on Macaulay, and probably constitutes the first major step in his modern reappraisal.) *History* : ch. 21, 'Effects of the Emancipation of the English Press'.

90. *History* : ch. 15, 'The Corporation Bill'.

91. 'Sir James Mackintosh's History of the Revolution' : 'Such was England in 1660....' *History* : ch. 4, 'Death of Charles II'. Antonia Fraser, *King Charles II* (London, 1979), 455 and n.

92. Macaulay to Napier, 20 July 1842 (*Letters*, IV, 47), 20 October 1843 (*ibid.*, 158). Macaulay to his sister Hannah, 5 October 1846 (*ibid.*, 313). Macaulay to Ellis, 17 July 1848 (*ibid.*, 370-1). *History* : ch. 17, 'Marlborough' ; 'Treachery of some of William's Servants' ; ch. 2, 'Character of Charles II'. H.R.Trevor-Roper, 'Lord Macaulay : Introduction', in Lord Macaulay, *The History of England*, edited and abridged with an introduction by Hugh Tervor-Roper (1968), 41, quoting S.R.Gardiner, *Cromwell's Place in History* (1902), 17. J.H.Plumb, 'Macaulay', *Men and Places* (1963). Churchill's criticisms run all through the text of his *Marlborough*, I (1933).

93. *History* : ch. 13, 'The Highland Army reinforced'.

94. 'History' : 'The perfect historian is he in whose work the character and spirit of an age is exhibited in miniature....' 'The Battle of Bosworth Field' was printed in *Macaulay's Lays of Ancient Rome and Other Historical Poems* with an Introduction by George Macaulay Trevelyan (1928).

95. *History* : ch. 5, 'Rapacity of the Queen and of her Ladies' (note to last edition corrected by Macaulay). Trevor-Roper, 'Lord Macaulay : Introduction', 32. 'Sir William Temple' : 'It is certain that, just before the Restoration...'. William Hepworth Dixon, *History of William Penn, Founder of Pennsylvania* (new edition : 1872), 'Note' and 'Supplementary Chapter'.

96. John Paget to John Blackwood, 22 February, 2 March, 1 April, 19 April, 12 May, 17 May, 11 August 1859, 8 January, 13

January, 3 August, 26 September, 7 October, 4 December 1860, 18 September 1861, 18 January, 19 February, 24 February 1862 (Blackwood MSS, National Library of Scotland : 4133, 4142, 4153, 4163, 4173). Paget to William Blackwood, 5 April 1859 (4142). I have also examined Blackwood's letter-book, and Aytoun's correspondence with Blackwood.

97. Herbert Butterfield, *George III and the Historians* (1957).
98. Raymond Williams, *The Long Revolution* (1965 edition), 76.
99. Lyttelton to Hart-Davis, 14 December 1961 (*The Lyttelton Hart-Davis Letters : Correspondence of George Lyttelton and Rupert Hart-Davis*, ed. and introduced by Rupert Hart-Davis, VI (1984), 141). The Cambridge prize essay on the life and character of King William III, ed. A.N.L.Munby, appeared in the *Times Literary Supplement*, 1 May 1969. *History* : ch. 25, 'Death of William'.

Bibliographical Note

I. *Manuscripts*. Trinity College, Cambridge. Macaulay's Journal (1838–59) in eleven MS volumes (with typescript transcription) was examined by me due to the kindness of Dr Robert Robson, who is editing it. Some leaves at the beginning have been torn away, apparently by Hannah, and relating to Margaret. Hannah also made some erasures, and Macaulay himself made some, the latter often easily deciphered.

National Library of Scotland. Blackwood MSS. This vast and rich collection relating to the firm of William Blackwood and Sons, of Edinburgh, and *Blackwood's Magazine*, contains letters from John Paget on his work for the Blackwoods attacking Macaulay, and copies of some Blackwood letters to Paget. Some letters from William Edmonstoune Aytoun throw additional light on the Paget essays. (I have also looked at the Aytoun MSS which contain some interesting lecture notes of relevance to Macaulay.)

II. *Letters*. Thomas Pinney's 6-volume edition of *The Letters of Thomas Babington Macaulay* (1974–81) is my leading source other than Macaulay's own published essays, *History of England*, and *Lays of Ancient Rome*. It is impossible to convey my gratitude to it. Apart from the texts, established with scrupulous care, it abounds in annotation and prefatory matter as thorough and judicious as could be hoped. The whole work is a masterpiece of scientific scholarship.

III. *Editions of the Writings*. The best 'edition' of the *Lays* is *Macaulay's Lays of Ancient Rome and other Historical Poems* with an introduction by G.M.Trevelyan (1928) : it also contains 'Moncontour', 'Ivry', 'Naseby' (but significantly not 'The Cavaliers' March on London'), 'The Armada' (with an early version), 'The Last Buccaneer', 'Epitaph of a Jacobite' and 'The Battle of Bosworth Field'.

Critical and Historical Essays received an annotated edition by Francis Charles Montague, an Oxford historian (3 volumes, 1903) : there is useful identification of some, but far from all, allusions rendered obscure by the passage of time and Macaulay's excessive respect for the learning of his readers. There is also much testy editorial opinion, useful in showing the nature of academic prejudice in 1903, e.g. 'the portions of *Paradise Lost* where Omnipotence directly intervenes are almost unreadable. But neither Macaulay's temperament nor his education was such as to render him sensitive on this point.' It is amusing to conjecture what Macaulay would have said of such comments. Montague says nothing about the textual alterations made by Macaulay between publication in the *Edinburgh Review* and in *Critical and Historical Essays* : in the case of the essay on Sir James Mackintosh's history of the Revolution these were considerable. I have used the *Edinburgh Review* texts as well as those in *Critical and Historical Essays.*

The History of England was edited by Thomas Finlayson Henderson, a Scots man of letters (1907) : the results are not brilliant, but are much more valuable than those Montague produced. Henderson also conveys the state of academic consensus on disputed historical points, somewhat uncritically. He is hardly felicitous in phrase (e.g. 'The victory of Naseby, 14 June, 1645, was won by the charge of the horse under Cromwell'). Charles Harding Firth's 'edition' (6 volumes, 1913–15), is simply the text with a wonderful use of almost every appropriate illustration, chiefly portraits, and with a greatly improved index.

Speeches has only one authorized edition, and while I examined pirated editions I made no use of them.

Miscellaneous Writings edited after Macaulay's death by Ellis (1861), include a selection of prose and verse from *Knight's Quarterly Magazine*, as well as some additional essays from the *Edinburgh*, and the five biographies contributed to *Encyclopaedia Britannica*. But the *Britannica* publisher, Adam Black, brought these last out as *Biographies by Lord Macaulay* (1860) with a memoir of considerable value on Macaulay's connection with Edinburgh by himself, one of Macaulay's strongest local supporters.

The best list of Macaulay's published writings is compiled by Thomas Pinney in *Letters*, VI, 289–302. It contains many items reprinted by neither Macaulay nor Ellis, and I have therefore used files of *Knight's Quarterly Magazine* (whose contributions by Macaulay's Cambridge friends throw light on intellectual and cultural influences on him in 1823–24) as well as the *Edinburgh Review*. The university prize essay on 'The Life and Character of King William III' was first published in the *Times Literary Supplement*, 1 May 1969. C.D.Dharker selected and introduced *Lord Macaulay's Legislative Minutes* (1946). The prize poems 'Pompeii'

(1819) and 'Evening' (1821) were published by Cambridge after winning their awards. The surviving fragment of the 'History of France' has been edited by Joseph Hamburger as *Napoleon and the Restoration of the Bourbons* (1977).

At the present time it is necessary to use secondhand bookshops to obtain Macaulay's works, apart from selections; this reflects credit on nobody. Dent kept the *Critical and Historical Essays* and *History of England* in print in their Everyman's Library until recently; presumably they let Macaulay go out of print as their contribution to the celebration of the tercentenary of the Glorious Revolution. Longman's had a 'popular' edition of the *History* (2 vols.), the *Critical and Historical Essays and Lays of Ancient Rome* (1 vol.) and the *Miscellaneous Writings and Speeches* (1 vol.) widely circulating in the 1890s, and it is probably the easiest and cheapest antiquarian purchase, if your eyes can read small print. Otherwise *The Collected Works* fetch high prices, being found in Hannah Lady Trevelyan's 8-volume edition of 1866, its 12-volume reprint as the Albany edition (1898), the New Cambridge 10-volume edition (with three more speeches) of 1900, and Henderson's 9-volume edition (1905–7).

IV. *Bibliography.* Apart from the invaluable material in the *Letters*, David J. DeLaura, ed., *Victorian Prose: A Guide to Research* (1973) contains an excellent if not wholly comprehensive bibliographical essay by John Clive and Thomas Pinney (19–30) which must form the basis for any student's further investigations. It covers manuscripts and bibliography; editions; biography and letters; and criticism.

V. *Biography.* My only serious criticism of the opinions expressed in IV above relates to its judgment on George Otto Trevelyan's *Life and Letters of Lord Macaulay* (2 vols., 1876, and subsequent new editions with some additional matter), that as 'Biography and Letters' it 'remains first and the rest are nowhere'. Modesty should have no place in this business. Admittedly, Pinney's edition of the *Letters* was yet to appear, but taken in conjunction with Clive's *Macaulay: The Shaping of the Historian* (1973) these must now be collectively regarded as Macaulay's leading biography. Clive's work takes Macaulay to his return from India, and ably establishes personal, social, political and intellectual influences on him. The rest of the story is easily followed from the *Letters*. As to Trevelyan, its attractiveness cannot be gainsaid, but it is wholly unreliable in its transcription of documents ; no letter should be used from its pages without comparison to the Pinney text. I have compared the original of the Journal to several of Trevelyan's transcriptions and have found him false again and again, whether by conflation of separate entries, unstated omissions, interpolations or rewriting. Trevelyan dominated historians' views of Macaulay for a century, and it is striking that so many hostile judgments of Macaulay flowed from admiring essays on Trevelyan's biography (e.g. Gladstone's, John Morley's, Leslie Stephen's, as well as J. Cotter Morison's sketch in Morley's *English Men of Letters* series, and the renewal of Matthew Arnold's attack).

Unhappily, the same verdict on fidelity with respect to documents has to be passed on *The Life and Letters of Zachary Macaulay* (1900) by Viscountess Knutsford (otherwise Macaulay's beloved 'Baba', Margaret Trevelyan) : Mr Christopher Fyfe discovered in her work the same pernicious practices employed by her brother when he compared her texts with original documents in the Huntingdon Library at Los Angeles. I assume that she adopted the method under her brother's advice. The book is a little wooden, but contains much material of value. Both books are an important repository of family traditions. It would seem that Baba's maternal preoccupations (and perhaps Hannah's maternal influence) must have stood in her way as regards writing her uncle's biography : he would certainly have preferred that she and not George did the work. George Trevelyan was much less close to his uncle, and honestly acknowledges such matters as his own tactlessness which made their last interview (a few hours before Macaulay's death) one of pain to Macaulay. He certainly shared Macaulay's beliefs in the integration of all races in the Empire, at least in his youth : his *The Competition Wallah* (1864) is a mordant attack on racial discrimination in India. Later editions of his *Life* include his extracts from Macaulay's marginal notes on English, Latin and Greek authors.

Macaulay's first biography was his sister Margaret's *Recollections by a Sister of T. B. Macaulay*, written in 1831–32. Nothing so beautiful has been written about him : Pinney (*Letters*, 1. xxviii) gets it perfectly, 'a charming mixture of affection, quickness of observation, and naive enthusiasm'. It appeared only in private printings (1864 and 1881) ; it should be published in its own right, and would probably delight any reader however ignorant of Macaulay.

VI. *Critical Studies.* Clive terms his own work a 'study'; hence it also enjoys pre-eminence here. Jane Millgate's *Macaulay* (1973) is a work of judicious analysis and deep research; it is presented a little like a run-of-the-mill case study, but few could approach it. Joseph Hamburger's *Macaulay and the Whig Tradition* (1976) is packed with ideas, many pursued into fascinating footnotes, and is a constant, constructive challenge to readers and non-readers of Macaulay. The Clive–Pinney essay (in DeLaura, ed.) sums up major literary examinations notably William Madden, 'Macaulay's Style', *The Art of Victorian Prose* (eds. William Madden and George Levine), and George Levine, *The Boundaries of Fiction*: I found both works stimulating without being over-persuaded by them. One has to make one's own theories. I was rather touched to find that the work to prove the most useful to me among the older studies was that of the winner of the Trinity College, Cambridge, centenary prize essay competition in 1900, an Angus-born student and future Oxford professor of economics, D.H.MacGregor. My admiration for Pieter Geyl as a great historian does not extend to his 'Macaulay in his Essays', in *Debates with Historians*, but it is a grim reminder that Macaulay can seem a bully to a Dutchman who has recently emerged from a Nazi concentration camp (to an Irish reader the bullying is merely amusing stage-Englishry). G.P.Gooch, *History and Historians in the Nineteenth Century*, is invaluable especially on writers other than Macaulay; this could be true of G.M.Young's various essays headed by that in *Daylight and Champaign* – Macaulay was also a creature of midnight and hemlock. G.M.Trevelyan's agreeable limitations in understanding his great-uncle may be found in his *Clio, A Muse and Other Essays*. Dom David Knowles probably produced the best single lecture on Macaulay to come from a working historian: it is agreeable that Knowles was one of the greatest medievalists of his time and that Macaulay was weaker on the middle ages than on any other time since Herodotus. G.S.R.Kitson Clark, *The Critical Historian*, is an entertaining case of a Tory High Churchman confusing his prejudices with historical objectivity, and criticizing Macaulay's use of evidence while perpetrating similar solecisms in the opposite direction. I could cite many comparable examples; academic historians writing about historiography can usually be trusted to misunderstand Macaulay.

Index

Indeed, the manner in which Temple mixes the historical and the fabulous reminds us of those classical dictionaries, intended for the use of schools, in which Narcissus the lover of himself and Narcissus the freedman of Claudius, Pollux the son of Jupiter and Leda and Pollux the author of the Onomasticon, are ranged under the same headings, and treated as personages equally real. The effect of this arrangement resembles that which would be produced by a dictionary of modern names, consisting of such articles as the following:— 'Jones, William, an eminent Orientalist, and one of the Judges of the Supreme Court of Judicature in Bengal—Davy, a fiend, who destroys ships—Thomas, a foundling, brought up by Mr Allworthy'.

Macaulay, 'Sir William Temple'

Note

I have not indexed Macaulay's life or his *History of England*. I have assigned dates for persons of even the most doubtful existence, on the principle that Macaulay's huge range of time-travel may benefit from an addition to the instrument-panel giving a chronological location which may also be useful for some of my own allusions: a tentative date in the future in one case may be withdrawn at the appropriate time if inaccurate. The Book of Job defied dating. Macaulay's usages of names are retained in conjunction with modern equivalents: his use of 'Lewis' for French Kings was apparently a concession to formality in his *History* as otherwise both privately and publicly he wrote 'Louis'. He might not have approved of this index, and indeed might have felt that every schoolboy knew its chronological information. Every schoolboy of my generation knew the answers are at the back of the book.

O.D.E.

INDEX